GUARDING OUR GUARDIANS

GUARDING OUR GUARDIANS

GUARANTEEING AMERICA'S VETERANS A FUTURE FROM DEPLOYMENT TO EMPLOYMENT

CHRISANNE GORDON, MD
WITH EZRA BYER

Published by Advantage Books, Charleston, South Carolina.
An imprint of Advantage Media.

ADVANTAGE is a registered trademark, and the Advantage colophon is a trademark of Advantage Media Group, Inc.

Printed in the United States of America.

10 9 8 7 6 5 4 3 2 1

ISBN: 979-8-89188-013-9 (Paperback)
ISBN: 979-8-89188-014-6 (eBook)

Library of Congress Control Number: 2026900879

Cover and Layout design by Lance Buckley.

01-23-2026 12:38

To all Guardians and their families
who sacrifice to protect our freedoms.

CONTENTS

PROLOGUE

When a nation asks its young men and women to put on the uniform, it makes a solemn promise that their service will be honored and their sacrifices will be met with unwavering care when they return home. That promise is not symbolic—it is the very foundation of the trust that binds the all-volunteer force to our country. And yet, too often, fulfilling that promise has been uneven, delayed, or incomplete.

During my time as secretary of the U.S. Department of Veterans Affairs (VA), I saw firsthand the extraordinary resilience of veterans—and the very real cracks in the system designed to serve them. I met combat veterans struggling with invisible wounds, such as traumatic brain injury and post-traumatic stress. I sat with families devastated by suicide, and I visited rural communities where access to basic healthcare required hours of travel. I heard from women veterans whose needs were overlooked and from young service members leaving active duty with little preparation for the abrupt shift to civilian life. These were not isolated stories; they were the reality of millions who served.

As this book details, the challenges are profound: over four hundred thousand traumatic brain injuries reported since 2000, nearly seventeen veterans dying by suicide every single day, and too many unable to translate their military skills into meaningful civilian careers. But there is also hope. Telehealth is breaking down barriers of distance. Polytrauma Centers and team-based care are redefining what recovery looks like. Whole-health approaches—embracing nutrition, mindfulness, and family support—are replacing outdated models of overmedication. Communities, nonprofits, and private employers are stepping up to partner with the VA. Progress is being made, but it is fragile and incomplete.

Why, then, do I feel so strongly about this work? Because caring for veterans is not charity; it is an obligation of citizenship. It is also the key to sustaining our national security. If future generations see that those who served before them were neglected, the all-volunteer force upon which our freedom depends will falter. Conversely, when veterans thrive—when they are supported in education, employment, health, and family life—they not only strengthen themselves but also their communities and the nation as a whole.

When our nation sends young men and women into harm's way, it pledges to them that their service will be honored with care, dignity, and opportunity when they return. That covenant is not symbolic; it is the bedrock of the all-volunteer force. Yet, in my years of work at the VA, I saw how difficult it has been to meet that promise in a sustainable and consistent way.

This book is not simply about policy or programs. It is about veterans—their struggles, their resilience, and their rightful place at the center of our national conscience. My perspective is shaped by the privilege of having led the VA, as well as a conviction that sustainable systems of care must transcend politics, budgets, and bureaucracy. Veterans deserve nothing less than a system as strong, enduring, and honorable as their service.

That is why I recommend this book to anyone who cares about veterans—because it not only tells their stories of sacrifice and struggle but also provides a policy road map for how we can do better. It challenges us to recognize veterans as national assets, to confront misconceptions that block their progress, and to support reforms that will make their care sustainable for generations to come. By reading it, you become part of the work of closing the gap between promise and practice.

-David J. Shulkin, MD

Ninth Secretary, U.S. Department of Veterans Affairs

INTRODUCTION

In some ways, I'm among the most unlikely candidates to write a book on *Guarding Our Guardians*. My private school education did instill certain military-like values, such as wearing a uniform, following orders, working in teams, respecting hierarchy, and avoiding conflict. But what I didn't have was the courage to truly commit.

However, back in 2007, my perspective shifted, and I transitioned from having little military involvement to becoming the founder and executive director of the Resurrecting Lives Foundation—an organization that advocates for veterans with traumatic brain injury (TBI).

This internal transformation started while I was sipping on a morning cup of coffee and reading the latest edition of a mainstream newspaper. The technology headlines, such as the rise of the iPhone, dominated that morning's news. But as I flipped through the pages, one headline leaped off the page and changed the trajectory of my life. It was titled "Veterans from Iraq and Afghanistan Malingering After Returning from War."

Malingering. What an odd word to use, I thought. Why would service members returning from combat exaggerate their injuries to avoid work? Intrigued, I began to read, and with each paragraph, an additional surge of righteous indignation coursed through my body.

The article reported that thousands of veterans were returning from combat with complaints of headaches, fatigue, and vision and hearing issues, along with memory and problem-solving difficulties. Many were off-balance, both literally and figuratively, and their loved ones barely recognized them when they returned.

The article suggested these service members were exploiting the system. But to me, I could instantly tell something deeper was going on. How could I tell? Because I'd experienced the very symptoms described.

The Day I Hit the Wall

In my first book, *Turn the Lights On!*, I shared the story of my TBI that occurred in 1996. Because I lived alone and was a workaholic, home décor always took a back seat to caring for patients and reading the latest medical literature. But with my younger sister visiting soon, I decided to pull several boxes of Christmas decorations and place settings from the basement crawlspace of my two-story suburban Ohio home.

Usually, I stuck to a small fake tree and enough ornaments to fill an hour of my time. As I sorted through the boxes, I reached the heavy-duty set of Christmas china—twelve place settings that were around 70 pounds total. Even with my sister in town, I decided that hauling that much weight upstairs for just one meal was not worth it.

The basement floor was covered with low-pile carpet, except for a polished concrete strip near the crawlspace entrance. I needed to push the boxes back in, using every bit of my 120-pound frame to shift the 70-pound box of china across the carpet and back into place. But when I reached the concrete, the box slid out of control.

My momentum carried me headfirst into the masonry wall surrounding the crawlspace door, and I knew immediately that this injury was unlike any I'd experienced before. I lost consciousness for perhaps thirty to forty minutes, and when I finally came to, I couldn't feel my right arm and leg. I couldn't focus my vision and was confused. For at least twenty minutes, I was too scared to move, worried that I had broken my neck.

Eventually, I decided to try crawling. My thoughts felt disconnected from my body, and when I managed to reach the stairs, I had to drag myself up one step at a time. I finally made it to the kitchen, where I grabbed the cordless phone. As I did, I suddenly realized it looked like a blank slate, and I couldn't remember what it was for or how to use it. So, I put it down and crawled to the front door, crumpling there in a heap.

Night fell, and I lay waiting. Fortunately, one of my friends was scheduled to visit that evening, and when she finally arrived, she took one look at me and thought I was playing a joke. It was clear she didn't understand the seriousness of the situation. My head was pounding, and when I tried to talk, no sound was emitted. Eventually, I found a pen and wrote "ER!" on a pad of paper. Writing was still in my muscle memory, and she finally understood. Within the hour, we were at the ER, beginning the long journey of understanding and recovery.[1]

A Different Story

For the next two years, I struggled to regain the life I'd lost, and even as I read this article about "malingering veterans" over ten years later, I was still putting some of the pieces of my brain back together. Unlike the brave warriors who were denigrated in this article, I wasn't

1 Chrisanne Gordon, *Turn the Lights On!: A Physician's Personal Journey from the Darkness of Traumatic Brain Injury (TBI) to Hope, Healing, and Recovery* (Corpus Callosum Creations, Ltd., 2018), 25–29.

injured in combat or training. No improvised explosive device blast, no life-or-death battle, just a clumsy accident.

And hours after my accident, while I sat in the ER and my CT scan came back normal, the attending physician (who was also my colleague) never questioned whether I was faking my symptoms. There were no op-eds in our local paper the next day with overzealous reporters claiming that Dr. Chrisanne Gordon was exaggerating her injuries to gain sympathy and get out of work. I was believed and treated with all the precautions necessary when your brain decides to disconnect from your body. And yet, in 2007, the brave Guardians who had traveled around the world to protect the freedoms I enjoyed were coming under scrutiny.

As I put down the newspaper, I felt that sickening pit-of-stomach sensation that comes with a life-changing epiphany. It was one I knew would reshape my world as dramatically as my brain injury had a decade earlier. Upon looking at my situation, I realized that I had many advantages that our military members did not.

I had the privilege of a medical degree, and those who examined me knew me, trusted me, and understood that I was incapable of faking my disability. I also had a two-year journey back to a new normal. However, I realized the aphasia I experienced from the TBI that left me unable to speak was the same sense of helplessness many brave combat veterans had experienced. And I also realized that perhaps one of the reasons God had given me my voice back was so that I could speak up for those who had lost theirs.

The Launch of Resurrecting Lives

Thus began my mission to rally the full force of civilian resources to repair and restore the battered brains of our nation's Guardians who carried the invisible wounds of the Global War on Terrorism. In 2012, our grassroots efforts gained official recognition when the Resurrecting Lives Foundation earned its IRS 501(c)(3) nonprofit status. From that moment forward, we stepped boldly into the fight for our veterans' futures.

Collaborative research funding models, such as the 2014 study at the Albert Einstein College of Medicine, demonstrate how non-profits can advance research on veteran care. This research was a turning point, proving once and for all that the blast injuries so many Guardians suffered in Iraq and Afghanistan cause damage to several parts of the brain.

Award-winning religious studies scholar Thomas Howard Suitt III estimates that "30,177 active duty personnel and veterans of the post 9/11 wars have died by suicide, significantly more than the 7,057 service members killed in post-9/11 war operations."[2] It's no wonder that in 2020, "the suicide rate among US veterans was 31.7 per 100,000, 57.3 percent greater than nonveterans, and suicide was the second leading cause of death for veterans younger than 45 years."[3]

In the United States alone, between four and six million new cases of TBI are reported annually, stemming from accidents, sports injuries, falls, and other causes. Among veterans, about 750,000 have experienced TBI from the Iraq and Afghanistan conflicts, alongside 115,000 living Vietnam veterans and 2.3 million active-duty military members who are also at risk. Today, it is estimated that roughly

2 Thomas Howard Suitt III, *High Suicide Rates Among United States Service Members and Veterans of the Post-9/11 Wars* (Watson Institute for International and Public Affairs, Boston University, 2021).

3 Jeffrey T. Howard et al., "Trends in Suicide Rates Among Post-9/11 US Military Veterans with and Without Traumatic Brain Injury from 2006–2020," *JAMA Neurology* 80, no. 10 (2023): 1117–19, https://doi.org/10.1001/jamaneurol.2023.2893.

1 million veterans require TBI rehabilitation services to help them manage and recover from these often-debilitating injuries.[4]

Armed with this research, I traveled to Washington, DC, and sat across from lawmakers, determined to link these injuries directly to the heartbreaking rates of suicide among our returning heroes. The Jacob Sexton Military Suicide Prevention Act, championed by Indiana Senator Joseph Donnelly, was born out of those conversations and signed into law. It formally recognized the connection between TBI and the devastating epidemic of veteran suicides.

Knowing that early treatment is the bedrock of recovery, we worked tirelessly to ensure that no veteran would be left waiting in the dark. A few years later, we secured a commitment from U.S. Department of Veterans Affairs (VA) Secretary Robert McDonald that every veteran diagnosed with TBI would have an appointment within two weeks of discharge. No more endless delays; just immediate, lifesaving care.

Since those first victories, our journey has grown into a movement. Through live presentations, our documentary *Operation Resurrection*, our experiential short film *Brainstorms*, and a relentless media presence, we have shattered the silence surrounding these invisible wounds. Each effort has amplified the simple truth that these injuries, left untreated, cost lives.

But we are not stopping there. Our mission has expanded to include events like Veterans Standing Together Across America, uniting communities in hope and healing. Our podcast, *Brainstorms*, named after our award-winning film, shares critical knowledge and stories of recovery that resonate across the country. Social media has

---

4 Robert Beckman, "The National Brain-Wounded Veteran Brain Drain," TreatNOW, November 2, 2021, press release, https://treatnow.org/knowledgebase/the-national-brain-wounded-veteran-brain-drain/.

become a lifeline, reaching veterans in their darkest hours and pulling them back to safety.

At the core of our mission is a profound belief that our nation's Guardians, just 1 percent of the population, are our most precious natural resource. They deserve not only our gratitude but every ounce of our ingenuity, compassion, and determination. We fight to ensure they receive what they have earned: access to healthcare, education, and employment opportunities that reflect their courage and sacrifice. Our work is driven by the conviction that these Guardians of our freedom should benefit from the vast pool of civilian resources this nation has to offer.

This work represents our commitment to every service member. You are seen. You are valued. And you will never walk this path alone.

Why You Should Care

Throughout this book, we'll dig deep into the disparities in care that our rural Guardians face every single day, and more importantly, we'll look at real-world, practical solutions to these challenges. In an age of global unrest, our future depends on a strong, committed military of men and women who can defend our freedoms and keep our way of life protected from the chaos of the world.

They volunteer their lives for us and for our country. At the very least, we can ensure that when they return home, they have the support to heal, regain their footing, and plan for a future that's worth living. I didn't see this mission clearly back in 2007 when I first read that newspaper headline. But now, I see it more clearly than ever, and I'm inviting you to see it too. Our veterans' lives—and yes, our American way of life—depend on it.

Our national security depends on supporting those who defend it. All those billions of dollars and all those shiny weapons do not matter if we're not taking care of the people who actually put those tools to use in our defense. Unless we demand accountability and continued change from the Department of War and the VA, as well as collaboration with civilian resources, that spending is a hollow investment. The people behind those tools are the ones who truly matter.

To be clear, these are not major overhauls we are requesting. They are basic needs that civilians enjoy at the expense of those who protect them. On the one hand, it's about our shared humanity. These Guardians are our brothers, sisters, neighbors, and friends. And on the other hand, it's about our very survival as a nation. When we don't treat TBI early, the long-term costs don't just add up; they explode. Homelessness, disability, incarceration, and lost productivity all radiate out and impact *everyone*, not just the veterans themselves.

Contrary to what you might believe, your voice in connection with others can make a powerful impact. As Margaret Mead famously said, "Never doubt that a small group of thoughtful, committed citizens can change the world. Indeed, it is the only thing that ever has."[5]

Our brave Guardians in the military are the backbone of this nation. If we don't take care of them, we're not just failing them; we're failing ourselves. Let's not let that happen. Instead, let's guard the very people who have given so much to guard us.

5 Margaret Mead, "Never doubt that a small group of thoughtful, committed citizens can change the world. Indeed, it's the only thing that ever has," Goodreads, accessed June 7, 2025, https://www.goodreads.com/quotes/1071-never-doubt-that-a-small-group-of-thoughtful-committed-citizens.

SECTION I

CONTEXT AND HISTORY

CHAPTER 1

THE REALITIES OF MODERN COMBAT

The battlefield today is much different from what it was in past generations, and nearly every soldier entering the Afghanistan and Iraq conflicts experienced a massive culture shock.

When our Guardians enter combat, it's as if they're yanked out of the twenty-first century and plunged headfirst into a world that's been standing still for centuries. Everything they know—the convenience of modern life, the familiar daily rhythms—suddenly doesn't matter. They find themselves in a world shaped by tribal warfare and ancient grudges, where survival is the only rule that counts.

This isn't like the wars of the past. During World War II, service members were shipped out from the American heartland to the fields of Europe. There were shared cultural ties and familiar places. But today's battlefields are deserts and jagged mountains. They are completely alien landscapes where service members are outsiders from the moment they arrive.

They encounter adversaries with generational knowledge of local terrain. And no matter how rigorous the boot camp back home, it can't begin to teach them how to read this land. Even the best gear doesn't stand up to the bone-chilling winters of Afghanistan or the sweltering heat of an Iraqi summer.

And then, almost without warning, these service members are sent home. Within twenty-four hours, they transition from combat environments to civilian life, where their surroundings appear normal, with suburban streets and everyday conversations. Their minds are still in combat mode, wired for survival, while the world around them has moved on.

Drones, Distance, and Danger

Modern combat seamlessly combines timeless challenges with the unprecedented advancements of technological warfare. On one hand, the grit, fear, and brotherhood of service members under fire echo across generations. On the other hand, technology has dramatically transformed how war is waged. In previous conflicts throughout history (excluding examples such as the Vietnam War), clear front lines and identifiable enemies were the norm.

Today, a US service member might be targeted by an enemy hacker or drone pilot a continent away. Since 9/11, the United States alone has used thousands of armed drones to strike targets in countries such as Afghanistan, Iraq, Yemen, and Somalia.[6] In Ukraine, for example, inexpensive drones guided by remote operators or algorithms are "twice as effective as every other weapon" in inflicting enemy losses,[7] a glimpse of the future of warfare.

Yet even as high-tech remote strikes become routine, troops still face up-close, gritty danger. Guerrilla fighters and insurgents hide

6 The Editors of ProCon, "Drones," *Britannica*, November 12, 2024, https://www.britannica.com/procon/drones-debate.

7 Gen. Valerii Zaluzhnyi, "How Drones, Data, and AI Transformed Our Military—and Why the US Must Follow Suit," *Defense One*, April 10, 2025, https://www.defenseone.com/ideas/2025/04/how-drones-data-and-ai-transformed-our-militaryand-why-us-must-follow-suit/404444/.

among civilians. The same patrol that is hunted by an unseen drone can be ambushed by an enemy behind the next wall. It's the combination of the worst of all worlds. The person far away who can take you out, and the person right behind the rock ahead of you. The lines between warriors and civilians are blurred, with women and children possibly being combatants or shields.

Of course, as someone who has never been in combat, I can't pretend to know exactly what that's like. But I've sat with hundreds of our service members who tell a similar story. One of them was Captain (Ret.) James McCormick, a highly decorated Iraq War veteran (three Bronze Stars and three Purple Hearts) and son of a Vietnam veteran.

"We experienced tribal warfare,"[8] McCormick told me, adding that "groups would kidnap each other's kids [and] murder children." In such an environment, service members adapt by mentally demonizing the enemy to do what must be done. This is juxtaposed with the realities of modern warfare. As McCormick added, watching an insurgent vanish in a puff of pink mist is a sight "nobody in the civilian world is ever going to see ... except in a video game."

New Weapons, New Wounds

Modern warfare's arsenal brings new wounds as well. Improvised explosive devices (IEDs) became the signature threat of Iraq and Afghanistan, with roadside bombs being triggered by something as ordinary as a cell phone signal. We never experienced blast injuries quite like these in prior wars.

Those powerful blasts, often causing violent concussions, meant many troops suffered traumatic brain injuries (TBIs) yet lived to return home. The good news is that improved body armor and battlefield

8 Captain James McCormick, interview by Chrisanne Gordon, May 29, 2025, for *Guarding Our Guardians*.

medicine have reduced combat death rates. But the harsh reality is that it has also left more survivors with invisible injuries. To this point, the Defense and Veterans Brain Injury Center has reported over four hundred thousand TBIs among US service members since 2000.[9]

"Some of the groups most disproportionately affected by TBI are the active military and veteran populations. While estimates of service members who sustained a TBI while deployed vary, sources indicate that the rates range between 202,481 and 320,000."[10] More than 185,000 veterans who get their care from the U.S. Department of Veterans Affairs (VA) have been diagnosed with at least one TBI.[11] Most are classified as "mild" TBIs (commonly called concussions), but even mild brain trauma can have serious long-term effects on mood, cognition, and personality.

McCormick acknowledges that on-the-job injuries were almost a given in the combat zone. "Our job dealt with life and death every single day,"[12] he says of his Iraq unit, which survived countless firefights and explosions. Some injuries are obvious, like when he was shot through the hand in an ambush. But others, such as TBI or combat stress, are harder to see.

McCormick describes how service members would press on through pain and trauma out of dedication to the mission: "This is my mission, and what's the alternative?" they would say. "I'm not going to lose the convoys and my American service members entrusted to me." That intensity and sense of purpose keep service

9 "The State of Veterans' Mental Health [2024]," Mission Roll Call, September 24, 2024, https://missionrollcall.org/veteran-voices/articles/the-state-of-veterans-mental-health/.

10 Nicole Doering and Stephen Reimers, *Untreated Brain Injury: Scope, Costs, and a Promising New Treatment*, abridged version (Reimers Systems, Inc., 2011).

11 "The State of Veterans' Mental Health [2024]."

12 Captain (Ret.) James McCormick, interview by Chrisanne Gordon, May 29, 2025.

members alive in war, but once the adrenaline fades, hidden wounds often surface. Depression, irritability, memory problems, and headaches haunt many TBI survivors.

These issues can fester, especially if a veteran is discharged "not fully well" and falls into the no man's land between the Department of War (DOW) and the VA without seamless medical support. In McCormick's words, "people [in Iraq] would hate you just because you were there. Some people loved you because you were there." That whiplash of being vilified one moment and valorized the next is a psychological minefield that today's Guardians carry with them. And many struggle to turn off the hypervigilance and aggression that kept them alive in combat.

Homecoming to a New Battle

Each year, about 200,000 service members make the shift from active duty to civilian life, a transition that underscores the changing landscape of the veteran population in the United States. Texas, California, and Florida lead the nation in veteran populations, with approximately 18.6 million veterans as of 2023. But by 2050, this number is expected to decline by 35 percent to about 11.9 million, with an average annual decrease of 1.65 percent. Of the current veteran population, over 5.4 million have VA service-connected disabilities, and nearly 67,500 are homeless, accounting for 10.6 percent of all homeless Americans and highlighting that veterans are more than twice as likely to become homeless as those who haven't served. In addition, over a million veterans live below the poverty line, and the current veteran unemployment rate stands at 2.8 percent.[13]

13 "How Many Veterans Are There? [2023 Veteran Statistics]," *VA Claims Insider*, August 7, 2023, https://vaclaimsinsider.com/how-many-veterans-are-there/.

When these Guardians return home, they face an entirely different challenge of reintegration into civilian life. In a Pew Research Center survey, 48 percent of post-9/11 veterans said readjusting to civilian life was difficult for them.[14] That is twice the rate of veterans from prior eras who reported difficult transitions.[15] This transition from battle-front to hometown can be jarring and isolating. After facing life-and-death stakes and profound camaraderie, veterans return to a society largely oblivious to their experiences.

I've seen it time and again. Young vets sitting in college class-rooms or starting entry-level jobs, surrounded by peers whose biggest worry is a bad hair day, while the vet is thinking about buddies who almost died or are struggling to keep on this side of the grass. This cultural gulf breeds frustration and alienation.

The more combat exposure and trauma a service member had, the harder the adjustment. It's no surprise that a majority of veterans with post-traumatic stress disorder (PTSD) or traumatic combat experiences struggle mightily with civilian reentry.[16] One awful outcome of this struggle is our national tragedy of veteran suicides. The latest VA data shows roughly seventeen US veterans die by suicide every day,[17] a rate about 57 percent higher than for nonveteran adults.[18] And that may be an undercount, as one analysis found veteran suicides could be 37 percent higher than VA estimates when accounting for misclassified deaths.[19]

---

14 Kim Parker et al., "Readjusting to Civilian Life," Pew Research Center, September 10, 2019, https://www.pewresearch.org/social-trends/2019/09/10/readjusting-to-civilian-life/.

15 Parker et al., "Readjusting to Civilian Life."

16 Parker et al., "Readjusting to Civilian Life."

17 "The State of Veterans' Mental Health [2024]."

18 "The State of Veterans' Mental Health [2024]."

19 "The State of Veterans' Mental Health [2024]."

These lost Guardians are often young, coming from the Iraq and Afghanistan generations, and their deaths speak to wounds of moral injury, isolation, and despair that were not healed in time. The risk of suicide is highest in the first months after a veteran leaves the service,[20] when the structure and identity of military life fall away.

The brain injuries and psychological scars carried by today's combat vets demand the same attention as physical battlefield wounds. "We are prosecuting and imprisoning veterans while denying them the care and consideration they need and deserve," warned former Defense Secretary Chuck Hagel, highlighting how often those who have served end up in crisis.[21]

McCormick himself strives to be an example of turning trauma into purpose, sharing his own story more openly now than he once did. "I used to be uncomfortable [talking about what happened], but I'm not uncomfortable now," he says, "because you become a big example for other people when you get propelled into that position."

Unfortunately, the DOW is experiencing a troubling disconnect between the amount of money it's spending and the lack of measurable improvement in reducing military suicide rates. In fact, active-duty suicides increased by 12 percent, rising from 331 deaths in 2022 to 363 in 2023. Despite this, it's betting without any solid evidence that an "unprecedented investment" of roughly $261 million in the 2025 budget will somehow reverse this deadly trend. That's a 30 percent increase over what was allocated in 2024 and nearly double the $150 million spent in 2021.[22]

---

20 "The State of Veterans' Mental Health [2024]."

21 "Justice-Involved Veterans: Honoring Service and Advancing Public Safety," National Conference of State Legislatures, October 22, 2024, https://www.ncsl.org/military-and-veterans-affairs/justice-involved-veterans-honoring-service-and-advancing-public-safety.

22 *VA Status Update*, Arlington, Virginia, March 11, 2025.

Thankfully, some are waking up. In the words of the VA Secretary Doug Collins, "The days of kicking the can down the road and measuring VA's progress by how much money it spends and how many people it employs—rather than how many veterans it helps—are over."[23]

From Rural Roots to Tough Roads

It's no coincidence that many of America's warriors hail from rural towns and small communities. Military service has long been a means of escaping limited opportunities for young people from farm towns and Rust Belt counties. In recent years, this trend has become striking. While only about 17 percent of Americans live in rural areas, as many as 44 percent of new military recruits have come from those communities.[24]

In other words, the American countryside and places often forgotten by coastal elites produce a disproportionate share of our volunteers. McCormick's own story reflects this. He's a West Virginia farmer who followed a call to serve. Many of his fellow service members were similarly country boys and girls. They return after service to those same hometowns, which greet them as heroes at the Fourth of July parade, but which often lack the health services and jobs needed for a successful transition.

It should be striking that less than 1 percent of Americans shoulder the burden of our nation's wars.[25] Even more striking is the reality that it's often the same families answering the call generation

23 Doug Collins, "Secretary Collins: We Owe America's Veterans Real Solutions," *The Hill*, March 6, 2025, https://thehill.com/opinion/white-house/5178785-secretary-collins-we-owe-americas-veterans-real-solutions/.

24 Meredith Kleykamp, "When a Simple Statistic Isn't So Simple: The Story of Rural Enlistments," *Veteran Scholars*, April 11, 2017, https://veteranscholars.com/2017/04/11/when-a-simple-statistic-isnt-so-simple-the-story-of-rural-enlistments/.

25 "The State of Veterans' Mental Health [2024]."

after generation. "It's in your DNA," says McCormick. "We're relying on a few really good families to hold up the entire country."

About 2.8 million veterans live in rural America and rely on VA healthcare.[26] These vets tend to be older and sicker on average than urban vets,[27] yet they live in areas with doctor shortages and few specialized clinics. Something as simple as getting to a VA hospital can require a three-hour drive for a rural veteran. Telemedicine and mobile clinics are helping bridge the gap, but rural vets still frequently report trouble accessing care. This is a challenge we must address because the communities that give us so many of our warriors deserve first-rate support in return.

Beyond healthcare, the economic impact of post-combat injuries can be devastating. Many veterans return with disabilities that make it hard to find or keep jobs. Unemployment among veterans with serious TBI or PTSD far exceeds the norm. One study of Iraq and Afghanistan vets found those with deployment-related TBI had unemployment rates three to five times higher than their uninjured peers years after returning home.[28]

In McCormick's case, he struggled with physical injuries and mental scars, yet he was fortunate to find new purpose in advocacy and farming. Not all are so fortunate. Too many drift into substance abuse or anger issues that land them in trouble. Both of these are effects of TBI. Disturbingly, recent veterans (especially those with

26 Maria Mercedes Rossi et al., "Rural Veteran Perception of Healthcare Access in South Carolina and Florida: A Qualitative Study," *BMC Health Services Research* 24, no. 826 (2024), https://bmchealthservres.biomedcentral.com/articles/10.1186/s12913-024-11241-3.

27 Rossi et al., "Rural Veteran Perception of Healthcare Access in South Carolina and Florida."

28 Hannah Dellabella, "Unemployment Rates More Common Among Veterans with TBI," *Clinical Pain Advisor*, June 17, 2015, https://www.clinicalpainadvisor.com/news/unemployment-rates-more-common-among-veterans-with-tbi/.

invisible injuries) appear more likely than civilians to be involved with the criminal justice system.[29] TBI causes changes in the brain that lead to substance abuse, anger issues, and difficulty processing.

Experts estimate that at least seventy thousand veterans are incarcerated in the United States today,[30] and many of them suffer from untreated PTSD or TBI.[31] These are not excuses for criminal behavior but a call for healing rather than punishment when possible. When combat trauma is at the root of a vet's crime, our society must ask: How can we do better by those who bore our battles?

Misconceptions That Hinder Care

Misconceptions about veteran care prevent effective civilian engagement. One of these is that the government or VA will take care of everything. However, this is simply not the case, and many of our brave Guardians are falling through the cracks.

Another myth is that someone who looks great on the outside must be healthy on the inside. There's this idea that if you're built like an athlete, you're going to be fine, but it's just not true. Sometimes it's the people who look the best who are doing the worst.

An additional big myth is that the war is over when a veteran comes home. The reality is that the war *never* truly ends for them, and it's extremely difficult to reintegrate into "normal society." People think because they were so successful in uniform, they'll be successful at everything else, but that's just not how it works. Most of them never even wrote a check before enlisting. No budgeting, no real civilian work experience. To think they'll just slot back into "normal" life is wishful thinking.

29 "Justice-Involved Veterans: Honoring Service and Advancing Public Safety."

30 "Justice-Involved Veterans: Honoring Service and Advancing Public Safety."

31 "Justice-Involved Veterans: Honoring Service and Advancing Public Safety."

The sheer loss of life that happens after these men and women come home is staggering. Since September 11, 2001, over thirty thousand active-duty personnel and veterans have died by suicide—more than four times the number killed in combat during the same period.[32]

This trend marks a significant shift from earlier wars, in which many service members did not survive to return home. Advancements in modern medical care have increased survival rates, leading to a rise in veterans living with TBI. "An estimated 17 percent, or almost 142,000, of the living US military veterans of the Iraq and Afghanistan wars currently have PTSD, and experts estimate that 35 percent may develop PTSD over time."[33]

Back in the day, PTSD was just starting to be recognized. It wasn't until 1980 that it was officially acknowledged as a brain health condition, five years after the end of the Vietnam War. During World War II, many who struggled returned home and lived in their family's attics, shut away from the world.

Families carried that burden quietly, but now they are overwhelmed. They're caring for young, strong, healthy men and women with brains that no longer work the same way. It's one thing to care for someone with visible wounds. But it's another thing entirely when you've got a twenty-five-year-old with TBI, no executive function, and a body that still wants to run at 100 miles an hour. War itself keeps the

---

32 Danielle DeSimone, "Concerns Rise over Military Suicide Rates; Here's How the USO Is Trying to Help," United Service Organizations, September 6, 2023, https://www.uso.org/stories/2664-military-suicide-rates-are-at-an-all-time-high-heres-how-were-trying-to-help.

33 Caitlin Kennedy and Sandy Wang, "Traumatic Brain Injury and Post-Traumatic Stress Disorder in Military Veterans: When Two Problems Collide," National Center for Health Research, accessed June 5, 2025, https://www.center4research.org/traumatic-brain-injury-post-traumatic-stress-disorder-military-veterans-two-problems-collide/.

brain in a state of adolescence,[34] and when that internal war continues after a veteran returns from combat, it makes it extremely difficult to immediately grow up.

Bridging the Civilian–Military Divide

I often emphasize that today's combat Guardians are this generation's greatest assets *if* we choose to invest in them. I challenge policy-makers, healthcare leaders, and CEOs to recognize the leadership, resilience, and talent these veterans bring to the table and to truly understand the price they have paid for our freedom. We owe it to them to close the gaps in care and opportunity, not just in words but in action.

For me, this means pushing hard for funding in brain injury research and rehabilitation programs. I see too many twenty-five-year-olds with blast-induced TBI left to languish because we haven't done enough. It also means ramping up brain health support, especially during that first year after leaving uniform, so no one slips through the cracks into despair. It means making sure that rural and small-town veterans don't have to drive 150 miles or wade through endless red tape just to access basic care.

Both Captain (Ret.) McCormick and I emphasize the urgent need for increased civilian involvement. *Americans must wake up and engage.* We can no longer afford to be spectators while only 1 percent of us serve and the other 99 percent of us enjoy the safety and freedoms that service has secured.

34 "The Adolescent Brain: Beyond Raging Hormones," Harvard Health Publishing, March 7, 2011, https://www.health.harvard.edu/mind-and-mood/the-adolescent-brain-beyond-raging-hormones.

Modern combat is brutal, fast, remote, and deeply personal all at once. But what happens *after* combat is just as defining. America's Guardians are coming home to a country that can and must do better by them. This is why we must listen to voices like Captain (Ret.) McCormick's, who can speak for those still out in the wilderness.

The mission now is to reintegrate and empower our warriors as community leaders, entrepreneurs, and healthy, thriving citizens. They answered the call to serve. It's time we answered our call to support them, ensuring that those who fought for us are never left to fight their toughest battles alone.

CHAPTER 2

THE BATTLE AFTER THE WAR

Few people enjoy the process of transition, yet, as you've probably noticed, it's inevitable. We experience transitions from school to family life and changing careers. You've likely faced at least one significant transition that dramatically altered your life.

But as difficult as it can be to move across the country or change jobs, the combat-to-civilian transition presents unique challenges rarely understood by those who haven't experienced it. One day, a service member is patrolling a hostile valley or leading a convoy through desert roads; the next, they're expected to seamlessly reintegrate into a placid civilian routine.

In World War II, troops spent weeks sailing home, giving them time to decompress with their comrades. Today, however, a modern warrior might be home from the battlefield in under twenty-four hours, plucked from a land of danger and dropped back into the twenty-first century overnight. Everything around them *appears* normal—the suburban streets, the chatter of people concerned with daily trivialities—yet nothing inside them *feels* normal. Their minds remain wired for survival, scanning rooftops for snipers or tensing up at loud noises, while life goes on around them as if the war never happened.

For our returning Guardians, this abrupt homecoming can be its own kind of whiplash. "The hardest thing in my military service was when I began the transition back to civilian life and realized I must learn to be what I never was: an official adult civilian," recalls one retired Army sergeant major who entered the military at age nineteen and served for twenty-five years.[35]

Stepping out of the military meant becoming a stranger in his own country, figuring out mundane basics such as managing a household or bonding with neighbors, all while his brain was still calibrated to the tempo of war. "Leaving from under that security blanket of the military culture was a tough thing," he admits, likening it to losing not just a job but an entire identity and family.[36]

Military service isn't just a job; it's a full-time identity and way of life. It dictates how one dresses, speaks, and even thinks. Service members entrust their lives to each other and build camaraderie that's difficult to replicate in the civilian world. When that chapter ends, they don't just change what they do during the day. They lose a community, a mission, and a sense of self all at once.[37]

Studies confirm that this transition often involves "important losses to identity, community, income, housing, routine, and career aspirations."[38] Not surprisingly, many newly separated Guardians describe feeling unmoored and alienated, and as one academic study

35 Jason Beighley, "A Veteran's Perspective on the Challenges of Transition," *VA News*, March 27, 2021, https://news.va.gov/86421/veterans-perspective-challenges-transition/.

36 Beighley, "A Veteran's Perspective on the Challenges of Transition."

37 Jeremy S. Joseph et al., "Reculturation: A New Perspective on Military–Civilian Transition Stress," *Military Psychology* 35, no. 3 (2022): 193–203, https://doi.org/10.1080/08995605.2022.2094175.

38 Joseph et al., "Reculturation."

put it, unprepared, confused, and dispirited by the abrupt drop-off in support and structure.[39]

In fact, between one-quarter and over one-half of post-9/11 veterans report experiencing "some" to "extreme" difficulty in basic aspects of life such as social relationships, work, community involvement, and even taking care of themselves day-to-day.[40] What might seem like "normal life" to everyone else can feel bewilderingly abnormal to a person coming out of combat.

When the Structure Falls Away

Why is this military-to-civilian leap so fraught with risk? A major reason is that society's support systems haven't kept pace with the unique needs of modern veterans. We prepare civilians for military service with thorough training. Recruits undergo weeks or months of boot camp and advanced training, where every hour is structured under the constant guidance of instructors.

The military breaks down a civilian's habits and then builds them into a soldier, sailor, airman, or Marine. By the time training is over, the service members have absorbed a whole new culture and identity. They know their place in a unit, they speak the language of their trade, and they're bonded tightly to those around them.

Now, compare that to the exit process. The military requires troops to attend the Transition Assistance Program (TAP), a series of briefings and workshops covering topics such as resumes, VA benefits, and job hunting. But as one analysis bluntly noted, "the assistance offered to help Veterans navigate this major life change is not as

39 Joseph et al., "Reculturation."

40 Joseph et al., "Reculturation."

robust in comparison to the training new recruits undergo when they enter the military."[41]

Whereas joining military service is a well-planned and rigorous process, leaving the military often seems like a do-it-yourself affair. Service members sit through a few days of PowerPoint presentations and are then largely left on their own to seek out any of the over twenty thousand government and nonprofit programs that are supposedly available to help them.[42] The burden falls on the individual veteran to figure out which programs to tap, which forms to fill out, and how to ask for help. It's a stark shift from the tightly guided life they've known, and it's no wonder that so many fall through the cracks.

Whereas joining military service is a well-planned and rigorous process, leaving the military often seems like a do-it-yourself affair.

In theory, TAP is mandatory and should be accessible to everyone. In practice, compliance has been spotty. A Congressional review found that up to 70 percent of separating service members did not complete all the required pieces of the transition program as designed.[43] Operational demands, such as a unit deploying or a soldier being needed on duty until discharge, can reduce the time available for TAP.

"The way TAP is currently formatted, it's a blanket program, and transition is such an individual process," says Army veteran Adam

41 Joseph et al., "Reculturation."

42 Joseph et al., "Reculturation."

43 Aaron Knowles, "Redefining Transition: A Veteran's Mission to Improve the Process for All," ClearanceJobs, May 22, 2025, https://news.clearancejobs.com/2025/05/22/redefining-transition-a-veterans-mission-to-improve-the-process-for-all/.

Peters, echoing a common critique.[44] A young enlisted Marine who joined straight out of high school will have different needs than a retiring Army officer with a family, and yet the same cookie-cutter syllabus is often applied to both. Without a tailored approach or personal coaching, many vets leave those classes with a binder of pamphlets but no real direction.

Crucially, timing is a problem. Some troops don't take post-military plans seriously until it's almost too late. And once the discharge papers are signed, the military's responsibility essentially ends. If a newly discharged veteran stumbles or becomes disillusioned a few months later, the DOW is no longer there to catch them. Unless they proactively reach out to the VA or another resource, they can fall into what one combat veteran described to us as a "no man's land" between the DOW and the VA, with nobody definitively accountable for their well-being.

As I've heard time and again from our nation's Guardians, the first weeks and months out of uniform are a perilous window. The structure and camaraderie that kept a service member going are suddenly gone, and if no new structure or support fills the void, things can get bad quickly. Indeed, research shows the risk of suicide is highest in the first year after leaving service. In fact, recently separated service members die by suicide at nearly twice the rate of US veterans overall.[45] It is the danger of a free fall before the parachute opens.

What do these dangers look like in human terms? Often, they start small: a feeling of not fitting in, frustration with "civvies" who don't understand, a creeping loss of purpose. A young veteran might find himself sitting in a college classroom surrounded by nineteen-

44 Knowles, "Redefining Transition."

45 "VA Launches 'Solid Start' to Proactively Contact Veterans During First Year of Transition," *VA News*, December 11, 2019, https://news.va.gov/69295/va-launches-solid-start-to-proactively-contact-veterans-during-first-year-of-transition/.

year-olds fretting about frivolous wardrobe issues, while he is haunted by the ghosts of buddies he watched die or numbed by monotony in the wake of adrenaline-fueled decisions that often had life-or-death consequences. That cultural gulf can breed real isolation and anger.

Many veterans miss the clarity of military life, when every day had a mission and your friends literally had your back. Now, back in hometown, USA, everyone seems busy with their own lives. The veteran's family and old friends try to relate, but their questions peter out after a while, and polite thank-yous on Veterans Day can feel hollow. Without intervention, alienation can deepen into clinical depression or self-medication with alcohol or drugs.

A New Form of Boot Camp

The good news is that awareness of this transition gap is higher now than it's ever been, and innovative solutions are being proposed from many corners, including veterans themselves, the VA, nonprofits, and even forward-thinking commanders still on active duty. One powerful idea came from a conversation I had with Dr. Hemant Thakur, a retired U.S. Army colonel who is now a practicing psychiatrist and trauma specialist, known for his work on PTSD and TBI in veterans as well as his contributions to mental health research and holistic healing.

He has guided hundreds of service members through deployments and homecomings, suggesting that we need to approach coming home with the same seriousness and structure that we approach going to war. In other words, why not create a "transition de-boot camp" that will deprogram veterans from the effects of war and PTSD and prepare them to be productive members of civilian life? His idea is that transitioning out of the military should be mandatory and fully funded while service members are still on active duty. Below are some steps that show how it could work.

STEP 1: PAID MILITARY LEAVE TO RECONNECT

First, every service member preparing to transition would get four weeks of paid active-duty leave to go home and spend time with family. This provides a vital chance to ground themselves emotionally and mentally before starting the next phase.

STEP 2: RETURN TO BASE FOR DECOMPRESSION AND ASSESSMENT

After leave, they'd report back to base for a minimum of four weeks of decompression therapy. This part would be required, and for some, it may need to be longer, depending on their injury or mental health needs. During this time, everyone would receive a comprehensive physical and brain health evaluation. They'd be given full access to their DOW medical chart, with a chance to update or correct any records. Aptitude and attitude testing would also be included to help guide them toward careers or programs that align with their strengths.

STEP 3: A FULL-TIME STRUCTURED DE-BOOT CAMP TRANSITION PROGRAM

This isn't a casual workshop. It's a ten-hour-a-day, Monday-through-Friday program that would be mandatory for every service member, regardless of rank. The content would be holistic, meaningful, and include the following components:

1. **Physical health:** Rehab, physical therapy, fitness assessments, and long-term wellness strategies.
2. **Brain health:** A systematic resiliency program to assist all war veterans to understand how they were programmed before and during the war and then teach them how to deprogram step by step in every aspect of life,

including techniques such as reconditioning, meditation, brain imaging, journaling, and anger regulation.

3. **Financial literacy:** Courses on budgeting, planning, and navigating VA benefits.
4. **Employment prep:** Real-world job readiness with guest employers (think Home Depot and others who actively hire veterans), interactive sessions, and hiring connections.
5. **Personal counseling:** Help with home life, moving logistics, and reentering civilian routines.

This entire process would be a coordinated joint venture between the VA and the DOW. It would be standard procedure on every base, designed and delivered with input from both military and civilian experts. When it is done, each service member would walk away with a *personalized transition plan* in hand. They would already be scheduled for a VA health intake, enrolled in a training or job placement track, and equipped with real strategies to manage the hypervigilance and overactive fight-or-flight instincts that so often carry over from military life.

Dr. Thakur's point, and that of others who have proposed similar concepts, is that intensive preparation is exactly what's missing on the back end. Army veteran Adam Peters, for example, envisions a transition boot camp where service members spend their final weeks or months of service training full-time for civilian life.[46] "You want to be a software engineer? Great. Let's get you some on-the-job training," Peters says. "You want to fly planes? Let's get you flight hours."[47]

In this model, each transitioning service member would be paired with a coach or counselor who works out a tailored game plan iden-

46 Knowles, "Redefining Transition."

47 Knowles, "Redefining Transition."

tifying career interests, lining up apprenticeships or courses, even tackling basic life skills. Rather than sitting through generic briefings, the service member would essentially muster each day for civilian prep, just like they used to muster for physical training and duty.

The program would culminate in concrete results, perhaps a civilian job offer or enrollment in an academic program, so that when the individual finally takes off the uniform, they aren't dropping into that free fall. They've got a parachute already deployed, guided by an experienced hand. It's an ambitious vision, but elements of it are already being tested.

Other Options

The Department of Defense (DOD) launched the SkillBridge initiative in recent years, which allows active-duty personnel within six months or so of separation to intern with civilian companies or trades while still drawing their military paycheck. This essentially allows a soldier or sailor to spend their last few months working for a private employer, attending a trade school, or even interning with a police department as a bridge to post-service employment.

Thousands have taken advantage of SkillBridge, and the program has shown promise in giving veterans a running start in new careers. "The DOD SkillBridge program provides active military service members with invaluable opportunities to transition into civilian careers through internships," one recent report noted, turning uniformed experience into a foot-in-the-door at companies that are eager to hire veterans.[48] In a similar vein, the U.S. Chamber of Commerce's Hiring Our Heroes initiative offers corporate fellowship programs that place service members

48 "DOD SkillBridge Success Story: Chris Kock," Job Center of Lake County, March 26, 2025, https://www.lakecountyil.gov/DocumentCenter/View/81762/DOD-SkillBridge-Success-Story-Chris-Kock.

in private-sector roles, allowing them to gain experience and build a network before they officially separate.[49]

Additionally, there are base-specific programs, such as the one at Fort Bragg in North Carolina. Fort Bragg, one of the military's largest installations, recognized that "one of the most stressful times for service members and their families is preparing to transition out of the military." In response, they set up the Career Resource Center (CRC) on base.[50]

This skills-focused, employer-driven hub brings civilian opportunities to the soldier's doorstep. The CRC provides employer-specific training, certifications, and counseling to help "veterans and warriors-in-transition secure a career before their tour of duty is complete."[51]

Still, as promising as these initiatives are, they currently reach only portions of the population. Many programs, such as SkillBridge and the Fort Bragg CRC, are limited to those still on active duty and require commander support or geographic proximity. VA Solid Start aims to call everyone, but some veterans don't answer the phone or remain skeptical of "cold calls" from a government agency. Notably, none of these efforts fully replicates the immersive, transformative experience of a true boot camp. They are steps in the right direction, yet gaps remain.

The goal is not to hand-hold veterans forever. This is a proud, capable community that doesn't want pity or permanent coddling. Rather, the goal is to provide a smarter launchpad consisting of an intensive boost at the beginning, followed by a tapering of support as the veteran gains stability and confidence.

---

49 "Corporate Fellowships," Hiring Our Heroes, accessed June 12, 2025, https://www.hiringourheroes.org/career-services/fellowships/internships/cfp/.

50 "Fort Bragg Career Resource Center," Columbia Southern Education Group, accessed June 12, 2025, https://csegroup.com/military/fort-bragg-career-resource-center/.

51 "Fort Bragg Career Resource Center."

Duty, Dignity, and a Unified Effort

The core problem isn't that our Guardians are incapable of adapting. On the contrary, anyone who's been through war has proven their adaptability in the most extreme circumstances. The issue is that we send them into a radically different environment without sufficient preparation or support, and we expect that individual heroics will carry them through what is fundamentally a team endeavor. But just as military members work as brothers and sisters to win in combat, no veteran should have to win the battle of transition alone.

Fixing this is not solely the responsibility of the military, the VA, or any single entity. It requires a whole-of-nation approach that treats the reintegration of veterans as a sacred duty and a smart investment. Policymakers are increasingly recognizing that seamless transition is a matter of national security readiness as well. After all, if young Americans see veterans struggling and suffering after service, who will volunteer for the next conflict?

> But just as military members work as brothers and sisters to win in combat, no veteran should have to win the battle of transition alone.

Recently, some in Congress have pushed for legislation to formalize a 360-degree transition program, essentially extending the DOW's responsibility for a service member's well-being for a period after they take off the uniform, until the VA and community supports are fully in place. Ideas include automatic enrollment of all veterans in VA healthcare for at least a year post-discharge, rather than requiring them to navigate a complex application process. Additionally, each transitioning service member could be assigned a sponsor or case manager who checks in regularly during that first year, similar to how military units assign sponsors to newcomers. There are also calls to improve data sharing so that, the moment a person leaves the DOW, their information and needs profile are handed off to the VA and local veteran groups, creating a warm handoff rather than a cold start.

Beyond government programs, there are roles to be played by community organizations, employers, and everyday citizens. Employers can expand initiatives to hire and mentor veterans not just as a patriotic gesture, but also because it makes business sense, given the leadership and skills veterans offer. Educational institutions can offer transition courses, and some colleges now have a one-semester "College 101 for Veterans" class that tackles study skills, cultural adjustment, and using campus resources. Local nonprofits and veteran service organizations are crucial as "connective tissue," helping veterans build new social networks, whether it's through a climbing club for veterans, a community farming project, or simply a weekly coffee meetup for veterans in the area.

These social bonds combat the loneliness and loss of tribe that many feel, restoring the sense of belonging that research shows is key to preventing suicide.[52] As one comprehensive study argued in 2023, we must view the military–civilian transition not just in vocational or logistical terms, but as a cultural and identity shift, essentially a process of "re-culturation."[53] Our Guardians need to find a new tribe and a new purpose; otherwise, that thwarted need for belonging and identity can foster despair.[54] The remedy is to actively integrate them

52 Joseph et al., "Reculturation."

53 Joseph et al., "Reculturation."

54 Joseph et al., "Reculturation."

into the fabric of civilian life, celebrating their strengths and addressing their needs, rather than expecting them to go it alone.

At the heart of all this is a simple principle: forethought and care. We know that transitions are challenging, so why not design a process that acknowledges this truth and mitigates it? All people go through big changes, yes, but when those changes involve the kinds of extremes our veterans have seen, we owe them an extra measure of foresight.

We rigorously train and equip our warriors for the battles abroad. Shouldn't we equally prepare them for the battles at home? This means starting transition planning early. From the day a recruit signs up, we should be thinking about their eventual return to civilian hood. As the saying goes, "There's no such thing as a 75-year-old soldier; everyone leaves the military someday."[55]

It means personalizing the help by treating each veteran as the unique individual they are, not a number or a stereotype, much as we learned to personalize care for TBI and other "invisible wounds" rather than apply cookie-cutter treatments. And it means sustaining our support, recognizing that while many will find their footing after a few months, some will need ongoing help for years, and that is OK. As a society, we must remain in it for the long haul, just as those veterans remained in the fight for us.

We've Been Here Before

The truth is, we've been here before. After World War II, our nation made the choice to invest in its Guardians through the GI Bill, and it paid off a thousandfold, lifting millions into the middle class and transforming our economy. Now, in the aftermath of the longest wars in our history, it's time to invest in a similar vision.

55 Beighley, "A Veteran's Perspective on the Challenges of Transition."

It's not just about money, though funding smart programs matters. It's about rethinking our approach. It's about treating that moment of transition not as an afterthought, but as the critical phase in a warrior's journey that it truly is. If we truly guard our Guardians during their transition, we will be more able to avert tragedies such as suicide and wasted potential, and we will unlock a wave of talent and leadership in our communities.

These veterans, tempered by war and devoted to service, can become some of our greatest civic assets: entrepreneurs, teachers, doctors, engineers, public servants, and community leaders. Many already have. They just need a fair shot and a steady hand as they navigate the bend from one phase of life to the next.

All people experience transitions in life, but for those who have worn the uniform, coming home is the ultimate transition. It is a bridge between worlds, one that we must build sturdier. Every veteran's journey will be different, but no veteran should have to walk that bridge alone or find midway that the planks are missing.

The war may be over for our Guardians, but our duty to them is not. Ensuring a structured, supportive, and dignified transition is nothing less than our moral call to arms on the home front, a battle for the lives and well-being of those who have given this country their all. It's time to win this battle, together, and in doing so, secure the promise that no one who serves will be left behind.

CHAPTER 3

WAR OF THE WORDS

One of the ways we can win this battle at home is by being crystal clear about the objective. Unfortunately, the words we use often work against this mission. Beneath the visible scars, many Guardians carry invisible wounds of war, and how we describe those wounds can be the difference between isolation and understanding.

In past generations, families often had no language for what was happening to their loved ones. For as long as wars have been waged, those who survive them have returned with nightmares, flashbacks, anxiety, and unseen pain. Yet, each era coined its own term for this timeless human reaction.

A Yale study examining fourteen million articles found that between 1900 and 2016, the media employed a carousel of labels for the same post-war symptoms, with each conflict spawning a new vocabulary.[56] In the early twentieth century, a trembling World War I veteran was said to have "shell shock." A decade later, similar symptoms in a World War II vet might be dismissed as "battle fatigue"

56 Yale University, "What's in a Name? Researchers Track PTSD's Many Identities During War," *ScienceDaily*, April 21, 2018, https://medicine.yale.edu/news-article/whats-in-a-name-yale-researchers-track-ptsds-many-identities-during-war/.

or "war neurosis." In veterans of the Vietnam War, some called it "post-Vietnam syndrome."

It wasn't until 1980, over five years after the fall of Saigon, that the American Psychiatric Association finally adopted a single clinical name: post-traumatic stress disorder, or PTSD.[57] This belated recognition came after decades of shifting euphemisms and reluctant acknowledgments. This "war of words" not only sowed public confusion but, as researchers argue, also slowed scientific progress in understanding and treating the condition.[58]

In short, society kept reinventing names for an invisible wound of war without ever fully confronting its reality.

From Mental Health to Brain Health

Dr. Jeffrey Bazarian from the University of Rochester has said publicly that for someone to develop PTSD, they almost certainly had a brain injury first.[59] Not necessarily from the same trauma; often, the injury predates the event. And once that brain is vulnerable, it sets up abnormal connections that make PTSD more likely when trauma hits.

When PTSD finally entered the official lexicon, it was a watershed moment. At last, the psychological aftermath of combat was being acknowledged as a real condition, not a personal failing or mere exhaustion, but a diagnosable disorder. This new terminology opened doors.

57 Yale University, "What's in a Name?"

58 Yale University, "What's in a Name?"

59 Doris McMillon, moderator, *After the Injury: Acute Care and TBI*, webcast posted by BrainLine and sponsored by the Defense and Veterans Brain Injury Center through the Henry M. Jackson Foundation for the Advancement of Military Medicine, accessed September 8, 2025, https://www.brainline.org/sites/default/files/video/transcript/BrainLineWebcast3_Transcript.pdf.

Vietnam veterans who had suffered in silence now had a medical term to legitimize their pain, and researchers and clinicians had a common language to rally around. The recognition was a crucial step forward. But if naming something is power, it can also be peril. Along with the word "disorder" came a lasting stigma that has proven stubbornly hard to shake.

The very label that validated veterans' trauma in the eyes of medicine carried the baggage of pathology. To a combat veteran, being told you have a mental "disorder" can sound like you are broken, defective, or weak. I've heard time and again from our Guardians who bristle at that word. "What do you mean I have a disorder?" they ask. "I'm having a normal response to a hellish experience."

And in truth, they have a point. The unintended effect of formally diagnosing post-combat trauma as a "disorder" has been to saddle it with stigma and shame that has become a real barrier to seeking help.[60] Too often, veterans avoid or delay critical treatment because they don't want to be seen as "mentally ill." And tragically, some of those who go untreated become statistics in the heartbreaking epidemic of veteran suicide.[61]

It's for these reasons that I've switched my vocabulary from *mental health* to *brain health* when veterans have suffered from TBI. While it might sound like semantics, there's a massive difference between telling someone they're "out of their mind" versus "out of their brain." That subtle shift in language opens up a world of hope. It tells the person, "This isn't who you are. It's something that happened to your brain."

60 "PTSD vs. PTSI: Science and Stigma: The Bases for Arguments to Change the Name," Itsptsi.com, accessed June 20, 2025, https://itsptsi.com/ptsd-vs-ptsi-the-arguments-for-changing-the-name/.

61 "PTSD vs. PTSI: Science and Stigma."

Brains Do What They Were Designed to Do

Simple as this sounds, it's sometimes difficult for our Guardians to make this connection. For example, years ago, when I was doing my second Level II TBI screen at the VA, I had a patient who was a young veteran. He'd recently returned from war, and I asked him one of the standard intake questions: "Would you say you're any different now than before you deployed?" This was a standard question on the VA Level II TBI evaluation.

This vet looked at me and said, "I don't know what you mean." I could sense he felt almost insulted by me suggesting he wasn't the same person today as before he'd left for war. So, I tried a different angle. "Let me ask you a question," I clarified. "If you'd spent a year in Disney World, just walking around the parks and eating Mickey-shaped pretzels, do you think you'd come back a different person?"

The veteran laughed and said, "Yeah, I'd be f***ing Goofy!"

I smiled, but I could also tell my point hit home. *Of course* he would be different. Who wouldn't be? Immersion in traumatic environments can't help but change you.

This was something I knew from experience. I grew up in Youngstown, Ohio, also known in the 1960s as Murder Town, USA. Factions of organized crime were so intense that, for a while, there were several "hits" making headlines all over the country.

Unfortunately, Youngstown briefly became a national poster child for crime and corruption, earning a reputation it couldn't shake for years. Back then, the number one way to take someone out was with a car bomb. We even had a name for it: "the Youngstown Tune-up."

One night, after a late shift at the mall, about twenty of us were walking to our cars. It was quiet and dark, with that eerie kind of stillness. Suddenly, in the parking lot, a guy turned the ignition, and his engine backfired. Without thinking, every one of us hit the asphalt. As we slowly realized what had happened, we got up, dusted ourselves off, and moved on as though nothing had happened.

In one way, our collective reaction was anything but normal, but in another, it was *very* normal, and our brains were simply doing their part to keep us safe. We weren't broken people. We were products of a broken environment. This true story became a revelation to my veterans. In fact, my vets pointed out to me just how important my upbringing in this Steel Town was in teaching me survival, as well as the importance of giving a *voice* to those who had lost theirs. In Youngstown, survival was as innate as cooperation and collaboration for a greater good.

PTSD is an evolutionary response. If your brain helped you survive something that killed the guy next to you, it doesn't want you to forget. It plays the tape again and again because it's trying to keep you safe. The problem is, the danger is over, but the loop doesn't stop.

One of the ways I often explain trauma to veterans is by showing them a model of the brain. I point to it and say, "Here's where your new memories are formed, hippocampus, and right here is where the trauma is stuck right now. Next to the hippocampus is the amygdala, the area where long-term memories are stored. That tiny distance is the path we need to travel to heal. You're not damaged. You're not crazy. You survived. And the fact that you survived means your brain did exactly what it was supposed to do."

I always remind them that no one has PTSD unless they have survived. The fact that they're alive means they've got strengths we need to build on, not suppress. I also use the term "brain health" instead of "mental health," because words matter. If you break your leg, no one tells you it's a character flaw. They give you a cast.

But with trauma, we've created this fog of shame and stigma. When you reframe it as a brain injury, it opens up a whole different kind of conversation. One built on hope and repair, not shame and medication alone.

Words Shape Our Actions

Words shape the lens through which society views our Guardians' struggles. That lens, in turn, can shape how society responds. We saw during the early years of the Iraq and Afghanistan wars what happens when invisible injuries are misunderstood. In 2007, when I first began sounding the alarm about TBI and PTSD in our returning troops, public awareness was scant.

There was a tendency to either romanticize the stoic, unflappable veteran or, conversely, to stereotype veterans struggling with PTSD as unpredictable and potentially dangerous. Neither caricature helped those who were hurting. What was missing was nuance and language that engendered empathy rather than fear.

> Words shape the lens through which society views our Guardians' struggles. That lens, in turn, can shape how society responds.

Over time, advocacy and education have begun to change this. Terms such as *invisible wounds* and *brain injury* have entered the popular vocabulary, often carried by veterans themselves, bravely sharing their stories. Each time a veteran stands up and says, "I have a brain injury from war," it chips away at the old stigma that mental trauma is something to hide. Each time a public figure or a VA official uses the language of health and injury instead of disorder, it shifts perceptions in the audience, even if subtly.

The words we use don't just *describe* reality; they *create* it. When we say someone "committed suicide," we invoke guilt, as if it were a moral failing instead of a tragedy. When we say *mental health*, we often picture something invisible and vague. But trauma lives in the brain as physical injury.

There are measurable changes in the amygdala, hippocampus, and prefrontal cortex. This is not just emotional. It is neurological. And yet we continue to speak as though veterans are fragile minds rather than injured bodies. That mislabeling creates misunderstanding and misdiagnosis. It also makes it harder to develop treatments that work.

One of the words that is overused in our society, in my opinion, is *hero*. In our current culture, it's thrown around constantly. Athletes are heroes. Actors are heroes. Anyone with a comeback story and a large social media following gets the label. But when we use that word too often, it loses its meaning.

The veterans I work with—the ones who left stable lives to serve, the ones who came home changed and kept serving through soup kitchens, support groups, and suicide prevention efforts—never ask for the word. In fact, most of them avoid it.

That's why, while I'll still use the term *veteran* frequently in this book, I believe *Guardian* is the better word. It carries the right tone. A Guardian is not performing. A Guardian is protecting. Guardians don't seek fame. They step into risk so others don't have to. They don't seek out a stage. They stand watch. It's a word that recognizes not just what someone did, but who they still are.

We Need to Humanize the Conversation

When we use the right language, we humanize the conversation—something that is desperately needed in this country. In some parts of the world, military service still carries significant cultural weight. In the United Kingdom, for example, it doesn't matter if you're a prince or a private. Service is respected and means something.

In the United States, that cultural connection began to erode around the Vietnam era. What had once been viewed as a shared national responsibility started to fracture along class lines. Programs such as McNamara's Project 100,000 pulled young men from the inner city (teenagers with few options and fewer resources) and sent them into combat. Meanwhile, those with privilege often found ways to avoid the draft altogether. That divide between the rich and the poor never truly healed, and we've been living with its consequences ever since.

Now, only 1 percent of our nation serves in the military. As the number of military personnel has declined, so has our civilian connection with their struggles. Most of us truly believe that all wounds of war are cared for with expediency; that the VA cares for them and our government looks out for their welfare after discharge from military service for the rest of their lives. However, that is not the case, and we, the civilian world, must accept our part in the task to assist with integration into a world that many of them have never entered—a world of new battles for healthcare, education, and employment. With tools to navigate as civilians, our Guardians are guaranteed the future that they deserve. When we no longer see them as part of us, we stop feeling responsible for them. We start thinking of their injuries, their trauma, their reintegration as someone else's problem. But that's not the truth. These are people who stepped forward on behalf of the rest of us.

They accepted the risk. They knew that they might not come home the same. They took on burdens most of us will never fully understand. That kind of decision deserves more than polite applause. It deserves care. It deserves systems that work. And it demands that we never lose sight of the human being behind the uniform.

Unfortunately, our systems often *do* lose sight. Walk into some VA hospitals, and you'll notice it almost immediately. I still remember the first time I entered a VA hospital in 2008 to begin my tour of duty conducting second-level TBI screenings. Uncertain about what to do, I approached the front desk and said, "Hello."

No one looked up, and without breaking eye contact with the screen, the intake clerk said, "Last four."

"I'm sorry?" I said.

"Last four," she repeated.

"Of what?" I asked.

With a look that said I was clearly wasting her time, she added, "Last four of your Social Security number."

For me, that small interaction was a small example of a much larger broken system. One that dehumanizes and relegates real problems to a number and not a name.

A Stronger Military Creates a Stronger Society

In the following chapters, I will break down how we can all play a role in reshaping the narrative surrounding healthcare, education, and employment related to the military. It's my belief that addressing these deep-rooted issues will not only transform veterans' lives but also create a blueprint for improving systems nationwide. These requests for better coordination of care will not be just my thoughts and recommendations, but also those of scholars, retired service members, physicians, and employers working in the veterans' space, who aim to provide better healthcare, education, and employment opportunities for all our Guardians.

It's no secret that many of our nation's youth are in crisis. And there is a reason Jonathan Haidt's *The Anxious Generation* won Best

Nonfiction in the 2024 Goodreads Choice Awards. We're seeing an epidemic of loneliness, depression, and anxiety sweep our country. Why is this the case? Much of it is related to brain health. As Haidt explains:

> The human brain contains two subsystems that put it into two common modes: discover mode (for approaching opportunities) and defend mode (for defending against threats). Young people born after 1995 are more likely to be stuck in defend mode, compared to those born earlier. They are on permanent alert for threats, rather than being hungry for new experiences. They are anxious.[62]

There's a lot I could add to this, but it's critical to note that the very issues we're tackling in this book can serve as a guide for the general population. By thoughtfully addressing our Guardians' needs and building robust, supportive systems, we can create successful blueprints for community-wide mental health programs, educational reforms, and employment initiatives. These improvements can foster stronger social networks, reduce isolation, and enhance feelings of purpose and belonging—not just among veterans, but across society.

> By guarding our Guardians, we are guarding ourselves, our American values, and our way of life.

In a real sense, by guarding our Guardians, we are guarding ourselves, our American values, and our way of life. The way this begins is through deep, honest, and humanizing conversations that neither idolize nor diminish. Ones that create a clear course of action without being hindered by fear or complacency.

62 Jonathan Haidt, *The Anxious Generation: How the Great Rewiring of Childhood Is Causing an Epidemic of Mental Illness* (Function, 2024), 93.

SECTION II

HEALTHCARE

CHAPTER 4

THE STATE OF OUR GUARDIANS' HEALTHCARE TODAY

It was early 2008, and the wars in Iraq and Afghanistan were raging. I began volunteering at a VA hospital as a rehabilitation physician to help diagnose the signature wounds of those who had served in conflicts. I'd heard some stories, but I largely expected a modern healthcare institution not unlike the civilian hospitals I knew.

I encountered significant systemic challenges. Veterans wandered the halls, unsure where to go. Nobody had explained how to schedule an appointment, where to check in, or what to do upon arrival. Communication was abysmal, and far worse than anything I'd seen in civilian practice. In those days, the VA system was notorious for poor patient communication. It has improved in recent years, but it's important to understand how deep the problems run.

Consider what a typical Guardian faces. They get discharged from active duty, still nursing injuries from an IED blast in Afghanistan. At discharge, their military healthcare essentially ends on the spot. The DOD is no longer responsible for them and provides no ongoing care, often without a clear plan for transitioning into VA healthcare.

The injured veteran is told to register with the VA for their healthcare needs. That's it. No warm handoff, no transfer of records, no appointment scheduled. Nothing. This abrupt transition is jarring for anyone, let alone someone coping with TBI or PTSD. When that veteran tries to enroll in VA care, they enter a maze of paperwork and phone menus.

In the 2000s, calling a VA hospital often meant navigating an automated system with nine options, leaving voicemails, and hoping someone would call back. If the clinic returned your call and you missed it, they might leave a message, but if you didn't get it, the appointment request often vanished. There were no follow-up calls, texts, or emails, unlike in modern clinics. The burden was entirely on the veteran to try again. For those with cognitive issues or anxiety, this was a huge barrier.

Even when an appointment got scheduled, the hurdles continued. If you arrived fifteen minutes late, the appointment was cancelled on the spot. I saw this happen numerous times. A veteran drove for hours from a rural area, got lost in a snowstorm, and arrived a bit late, only to be turned away, with the next opening being months away. There was no leeway or understanding for what they'd been through.

I'll never forget tracking down one young man after he missed his slot. The clinic had simply marked him a no-show and moved on. In fact, I wasn't even allowed to call him, as reaching out to a patient was deemed "violating their privacy." But I called anyway, because I was worried. This veteran hadn't just missed an appointment; he had nearly missed *hope*. When I reached him by phone, he admitted that after getting lost and being turned away, he felt so defeated that he contemplated giving up on getting help altogether.

Unfortunately, stories like this were frequent. Back then, VA staff were often so caught up in regulations that they overlooked liability. There was no liability at the VA. This basic courtesy was neglected. As one administrator admonished me, "Dr. Gordon, we don't coddle people here."

But there's a difference between coddling and common courtesy. A simple reminder call or a rescheduled appointment is not coddling; it's a caring gesture. But too often, that caring was absent in favor of strict regulations that seemed to be at odds with the competitiveness of civilian healthcare systems, which vie to attract patients based on the quality of care they offer. The atmosphere could feel like a grim Social Security office rather than a place of healing. Little wonder that some of our Guardians would rather suffer in silence than brave the VA's waiting rooms.

A Broken System

I vividly recall a twenty-one-year-old veteran who walked into my exam room, looking shaken. Before I could begin, he gazed out the window and said softly, "I almost walked into traffic on the freeway before coming here. It'd be easier to get run over than to tell my story again." This young man had survived eight IED blasts during his deployment and, in my medical opinion, was clearly suffering from TBI.

Yet, when I escorted him to the mental health unit downstairs in hopes of immediate help, they scheduled him for an appointment six weeks out. Six weeks—for a person whom I perceived as a suicidal young veteran with a brain injury. I was reminded that I was not experienced working with veterans like they were, and yet, I was concerned. Because he had already spent twenty minutes talking to the mental health intake, the staff told me he had "used up" the time for my consult and would have to come back another day for me to evaluate his TBI.

Not on my watch. I brought him back to my office and completed my neuro exam and TBI workup right then. Before he left, I handed him my personal card with my phone number. I gave him a task for the evening to look up on the computer the articles written about TBI as the signature wound of the wars in Iraq and Afghanistan. I told him we would discuss it at ten o'clock that night, which we did.

I told him to call me anytime over the next six weeks if he needed support while we waited for that psychiatry appointment, and I intermittently checked in on him, or he would check in with me. Technically, that was also against the unwritten rules, as doctors weren't supposed to give out personal contact info. But how could I not? I was a civilian rehab physician, essentially volunteering my TBI rehab skills while the system was overloaded. I had given my personal contact information to my patients in my private practice, and this veteran was one of them that day—and so he would continue to be for the next few weeks. He taught me more than I ever learned in textbooks about depression and survivors' guilt, and I am very thankful for his mentorship.

Experiences like this opened my eyes to a devastating truth. During my first year of volunteering at the VA, two days a month, I experienced more system failures than I had in my civilian medical practice. The quality of doctors, nurses, and healthcare staff was not the issue. They were dedicated, skilled, and compassionate. The issue was the system: a tangle of bureaucracy, poor communication, and outdated processes, especially records and appointment keeping. A common saying inside VA was, "If you've seen one VA, you've seen one VA."

In other words, every VA hospital operated in its own silo, with its own quirks, and little consistency or communication among them. There was no perceived standard playbook ensuring that a veteran in Seattle and a veteran in Indianapolis received the same level of care or customer service. Everything depended on local leadership and legacy habits. This fragmentation extended all the way down to medical records, which turned out to be a *huge* problem.

The Gap Between the DOW and the VA

The disconnect between the DOW and the VA healthcare systems has been one of the most pernicious problems. When a service member is on active duty, their medical care is handled by the DOW's system. But the day they take off the uniform, responsibility shifts to the VA. Historically, the medical records of the two systems did not automatically transfer.

Shockingly, a veteran's comprehensive medical file from years of service would not routinely make it to the VA. Most often, it seemed, veterans started from scratch as a new patient at the VA, as if their combat injuries had no history that had been consistently logged and verified in all cases. Critical details, such as a spinal fracture from a hard parachute landing, documented blast exposures, and the prescriptions that were working, might not be known to their new VA doctors. And, to my knowledge, they did not receive any records to hand carry, and no records were embedded on a jump drive.

Why? A big reason was incompatible record systems. The VA's health record software (called VistA) was developed in-house decades ago and evolved separately at each of the 150+ VA medical centers. Incredibly, there were over 130 different versions of VistA in use across the country, each one customized and tweaked locally.

One VA hospital's system often couldn't directly share data with another's, let alone with the former DOD. By 2017, officials estimated that updating and unifying VA's aging system to modern standards would cost around $19 billion over ten years, and it still wouldn't fully achieve the seamless interoperability with DOD that was needed.[63] In essence, it was actually cheaper and easier to scrap the whole thing

63 U.S. Government Accountability Office, *Preparations for Transitioning to a New Electronic Health Record* (GAO, June 12, 2018), GAO-18-636T, 10.

and adopt the same commercial electronic health record that the DOD was moving to.

For veterans, the impact of this gap was deeply personal. I met one Guardian, for example, who had been on a stable medication regimen for depression and PTSD while in the Army. But when he showed up at the VA after discharge, the doctors there did not have his DOD records.

Unnecessary delays and interruptions in treatment followed while they tried to reassess and recreate his history. David Shulkin, MD, a medical leader who later became our ninth VA secretary, said he had heard “too many stories” of exactly this scenario: a veteran’s care plan falling apart because of missing records and lack of coordination when moving from the DOD to the VA.

Shulkin made it a priority to fix this issue, pushing for a single integrated records system so that “the VA and the DOD speak the same language” in healthcare. That initiative finally began in 2018, and although it’s not yet complete, the goal is for a service member’s medical history to follow them digitally from the battlefield to the VA clinic one day.

Over the last decade, progress has been made. The VA and the newly renamed DOW are now attempting to share a common electronic health record system. Legislation has mandated better transition assistance for departing service members. But gaps remain.

To this day, veterans often report that they must personally ensure paperwork is transferred and re-explain their entire medical history to each new provider. And disturbingly, some veterans are entirely locked out of VA healthcare because of the type of discharge they received from the military. Approximately 15–16 percent of service members do not receive an “Honorable” discharge. Some receive “General Under Honorable Conditions” and a smaller portion (around 5 percent) receive "Other Than Honorable (OTH)" discharges.[64]

Historically, the VA was mandated by Congress not to provide health services to those with OTH discharges, under the idea that their misconduct in service disqualified them. In reality, many of those cases involve minor infractions or problems that were themselves symptoms of war-related trauma (such as undiagnosed PTSD leading to behavioral issues). Yet, these veterans were being shown the door when they tried to get care.

Inside the VA Health System

To understand our Guardians' healthcare today, one must grasp not only the structural gaps but also the internal culture and incentives of the VA health system. The Veterans Health Administration is America's largest integrated healthcare system, serving over six million vets a year. It runs on federal budgets and policies that differ markedly from the private sector.

At the VA clinic, however, when I recommended cognitive rehabilitation therapy for a young veteran with TBI, the response from the pharmacy staff was chilling. He told me bluntly, "Your therapy would cost $10,000 a year. Zoloft is five cents a pill, Paxil is ten cents, and Seroquel is maybe twenty-five cents. It's easier for us to treat them with medications than with therapies." In that algebra, a complex brain injury was reduced to treatment with less expensive psychiatric drug prescriptions to save money, rather than therapies. This fit with our society's whole "take a pill" philosophy. It took several years, but that philosophy changed—only after several psychiatric experts

64 Stephanie Brooks Holliday and Eric R. Pedersen, "The Association Between Discharge Status, Mental Health, and Substance Misuse Among Young Adult Veterans," *Psychiatry Research* 256 (October 2017): 428–34, https://www.ncbi.nlm.nih.gov/pmc/articles/PMC5603389/.

on both sides of the treating equation, civilian and VA, recognized the benefits of therapies, especially holistic therapies, over medication. Yet, the suicide rates of young veterans on multiple medications were alarming—the nation was learning that TBI was *not* successfully treated by medications alone.

Medications certainly have their place, but they do not repair a brain injury. What they do, unfortunately, is sedate symptoms, often at the cost of side effects. Sedating a veteran is not the same as *rehabilitating* a veteran.

The human cost of this approach became painfully apparent. Throughout the 2010s, veteran advocates sounded the alarm about overmedication in VA patients. Powerful drugs such as Seroquel (an antipsychotic often given for insomnia or anxiety) were handed out liberally. Many Guardians I encountered were on a cocktail of six, eight, even twelve pills per day—a practice sometimes grimly nicknamed "combat cocktail."

Yet, as TBI screening developed in the early 2000s, very few had access to intensive therapy, neurological rehab, or holistic treatments. Some of the tragic outcomes in this era speak for themselves. Veteran suicide rates climbed. It was not uncommon to hear that a veteran who died by suicide had multiple psychotropic drugs in his system. In some of the most heartbreaking cases, veterans in crisis felt so desperate that they took their lives on the very doorsteps of VA facilities.

In New Orleans, a whistleblower raised alarming concerns that the VA underdiagnosed TBI among Iraq and Afghanistan veterans. Dr. Frederic Sautter, who led the family mental health program, found that while VA protocol in other centers led to TBI diagnoses in 60–80 percent of veterans who screened positive, only 18 percent received a diagnosis at the New Orleans VA—one neuropsychologist diagnosed just

9 percent of such cases.[65] This stark disparity meant many vets with blast exposure and classic symptoms such as memory loss, headaches, and PTSD were not referred for further evaluation or treatment.

A tragic case exemplifies the consequences: Sgt. Daniel Murphy, a decorated combat engineer exposed to an IED, screened positive in June 2017 but was not officially diagnosed. Despite recording memory issues, there was no diagnosis of TBI, only PTSD and depression. Hours later, Murphy died by suicide at age thirty-two—leaving his family to blame systemic neglect.[66]

Efforts by Dr. Sautter and nurse Priscilla Peltier to re-evaluate hundreds of veterans were not successful. Peltier described an internal list of vets "slipped through the cracks," but her proposal was shut down by the department chief, who reportedly said, "lose the list."[67] Their concerns prompted an internal VA medical inspector review in March 2019, but the official investigation results were never publicly released. The VA later dismissed the findings, attributing them to flawed data and claiming compliance with the recommendations; however, at least one veteran told a *CBS News* crew that covered this story as part of a Veterans Day revelation in 2020 that he still hadn't been contacted for follow-up care.[68]

Dr. Shulkin's memoir about his time as VA Secretary is tellingly titled *It Shouldn't Be This Hard to Serve Your Country*. That title carries a double meaning. First, it shouldn't be so hard for veterans to get the care they've earned. And second, it shouldn't be so hard

65 Jim Axelrod and Michael Kaplan, "Whistleblower: VA Failed to Properly Assess Hundreds of Veterans for Traumatic Brain Injuries," *CBS News*, November 12, 2020, https://www.cbsnews.com/news/veterans-traumatic-brain-injuries-va-new-orleans-whistleblower/.

66 Axelrod and Kaplan, "Whistleblower."

67 Axelrod and Kaplan, "Whistleblower."

68 Axelrod and Kaplan, "Whistleblower."

for good people inside the VA to do the right thing. Shulkin, who came from leading private hospitals, seemed taken aback by the bureaucratic inertia and infighting he encountered.

He noted, for example, that "the system incentivizes disability, when it should be incentivizing health and well-being."[69] By this, he meant that the VA's benefits and compensation structure actually rewards our Guardians for being sicker, as you get paid disability compensation if you have service-connected conditions. However, it offers little reward for recovering or becoming independent.

In fact, a veteran who works hard to rehabilitate and improve their condition might be reviewed and *lose* some of their disability rating (and payments). Nobody intends to punish someone for getting better, but the system's design inadvertently sends that message. This is a fundamental tension: Taking care of those injured in service is a sacred obligation, yet we must be careful to support their rehabilitation, not consign them to a lifetime identity as "disabled veterans."

Signs of Progress

Despite the numerous challenges, it's essential to acknowledge that veterans' healthcare has improved in many respects over the past decade. Public scrutiny and bipartisan pressure following the mid-2010s scandals compelled the VA to implement changes. Many dedicated people on the inside and allies on the outside have worked tirelessly to turn things around.

One major positive development was the creation of Polytrauma Centers—specialized rehabilitation centers for the most severely injured veterans, often those with multiple traumatic injuries, including

69 Benjamin Krause, "Secretary Wants to Redo VA Disability, Present System 'Not Sustainable,'" *DisabledVeterans.org*, June 23, 2017 (updated April 14, 2025), sec. "Secretary Wants to Redo VA Disability ..." (quoting Secretary David Shulkin), para. 3.

TBI. David Cifu, MD, a physical medicine and rehabilitation physician, was instrumental in establishing these collaborative centers as our Guardians returned to the civilian world struggling with significant and multiple injuries. The VA partnered with top-tier civilian hospitals and universities to establish five Polytrauma Rehabilitation Centers in Minneapolis (Minnesota), Palo Alto (California), Richmond (Virginia), Tampa (Florida), and San Antonio (Texas).

These centers are attached to major medical institutions and leverage cutting-edge expertise. For example, the San Antonio Polytrauma Center works closely with the military's Level I trauma hospital there, and the Palo Alto Polytrauma Center is affiliated with Stanford University. At these facilities, Guardians can receive team-based care from neurologists, rehabilitation physicians, psychologists, physical therapists, and other specialists. The difference in outcomes for patients who access Polytrauma Centers has been phenomenal.

I've seen Guardians with severe brain injuries learn to walk and speak again, to manage their pain and PTSD, and to find a path forward. It's a stark contrast to the fragmented care a veteran might receive at a smaller VA clinic or even a civilian hospital in a rural area, rather than a teaching hospital. You need brain experts in diagnostics, surgery, and rehabilitation, and these specialists are typically found at tertiary hospitals, where the necessary equipment and staffing are available. The lesson is clear: Integrating VA care with the best of America's civilian healthcare system is designed to coordinate and improve the quality of care for our most injured Guardians. Where the VA has formed collaborations with major research hospitals, veterans have benefited immensely. This Polytrauma model, under the direction of Physical Medicine and Rehabilitation Specialist Dr. David Cifu, remains a breakthrough concept that has elevated TBI care in the VA as well as the civilian healthcare system.

Another area of progress is telehealth and rural outreach. The VA, recognizing that nearly half of post-9/11 veterans live in rural areas, ramped up telemedicine programs to reach vets who live far from VA centers. During the 2010s, the VA became a leader in telehealth out of necessity, conducting over a million telehealth visits annually by 2018. This included tele-mental health (therapy or psychiatry sessions over video) and even pilot programs for remote rehabilitation exercises.

> Integrating VA care with the best of America's civilian health-care system is designed to coordinate and improve the quality of care for our most injured Guardians.

But behind the numbers, real progress was happening too. The VA established a national telehealth center, and during the COVID-19 pandemic, it expanded video visits dramatically. For a veteran with mobility issues or far from a clinic, telehealth can be life-changing. The key now is to improve broadband access in rural communities and ensure that these remote services are truly interactive and therapeutic. Bringing care to the patient, rather than requiring travel, is now a VA mantra, and it's the right one.

Perhaps the most meaningful shift has been the VA's gradual adoption of a more holistic view of veteran health. There's a growing acknowledgment that invisible wounds such as TBI and PTSD require more than a quick pill fix.

For example, the VA now screens every new combat veteran for TBI and has built a network of TBI clinics. It has started hiring more neurologists and rehab specialists, not just psychiatrists, to treat post-concussion symptoms. There's also a movement toward "whole health," offering alternatives such as mindfulness, yoga, and art therapy, while emphasizing nutrition and exercise as part of treatment. In the past, these might have been dismissed as fluff, but now the VA is funding such programs because evidence shows they help.

On the policy front, Congress and VA leadership have enacted reforms to increase accountability and choice. After the waitlist scandal of 2014, when it was revealed that some VA managers hid appointment delays, leading to veteran deaths, an Accountability Act was passed to make it easier to remove negligent employees. Whistleblower protections were strengthened.

The Veterans Access, Choice, and Accountability Act of 2014, and its expansion in the VA MISSION Act of 2018, gave veterans the right to use private healthcare paid for by VA if the VA couldn't provide timely care or if travel to a VA facility was too burdensome. This was a controversial step, and some feared it was a push to privatize the VA, but it has been a godsend for many veterans who can now see a local doctor or specialist when VA wait times are long.

For instance, a veteran in a rural town can get approval to see a community doctor rather than drive three hours to the nearest VA hospital. The VA still coordinates and pays for that care, maintaining oversight. While not perfect, these community care options add flexibility and have spurred the VA to improve services, encouraging veterans to choose VA facilities.

It's also worth noting the intangible but significant change: Public awareness and bipartisan support for our Guardians' health are at an all-time high. Today, unlike in some past eras, no one is openly arguing that caring for veterans is too costly or not our responsibility. In fact, funding for VA healthcare has increased steadily. The VA budget is now over $100 billion for healthcare alone, reflecting the nation's commitment to those who have served.

And from Republican to Democrat, there is broad agreement on the need to get this right. I personally witnessed senators of both parties come together after hearing about the struggles veterans faced. Their interventions helped force improvements at my local VA and others. This kind of united front is crucial because it means that when VA leadership or bureaucracy falls short, elected officials will apply pressure.

So, while real and very problematic issues remain, I'm thankful that our Guardians' healthcare is not a partisan issue; it's an American issue. We're all in this together. I'm thankful the VA has made so many changes in the last decade. There has been significant progress considering the bureaucracy that has existed, and I am in awe of great VA leaders such as Secretary Robert McDonald (2014–2017) and Secretary David Shulkin, MD (undersecretary 2014–2017; secretary 2017–2018), who accomplished so much forward movement in technology implementation, communications, and holistic treatments during their time in office. The VA I witnessed in 2008–2009 was changing rapidly for the better during these critical years of the Global War on Terrorism (GWOT).

CHAPTER 5

IT SHOULDN'T TAKE A GENERAL

One of the most persistent themes echoed by experts is the critical need for a seamless handoff of medical records and continuity of care as service members move from the former DOD into the VA system.

Brig. Gen. (Ret.) Carol Ann Fausone has witnessed this breakdown from the policy level down to individual cases. She spent years at DOD Health Affairs and in state veterans' affairs, where she learned how incompatible record systems and bureaucracy turned the simple act of transferring a file into a monumental challenge. I had the privilege to interview her, and as she told me, "It's unacceptable that a medic in Afghanistan often knew more about a soldier's wounds than the VA doctor back home, simply because the systems don't talk to each other."[70]

Fausone emphasizes that this gap isn't just a technical glitch, but a life-threatening lapse in care. "A veteran shouldn't have to hand-carry paper records from base to the VA in the twenty-first century," she told me firmly. Yet for too long, that was the norm.

70 Brigadier General Carol Ann Fausone, interview by Chrisanne Gordon, *Guarding Our Guardians*.

We discussed how Guardians, like one former veteran on a stable medication regimen for PTSD, saw their treatment plan fall apart when the VA couldn't access their DOD records. "Imagine fighting for your country, only to have to fight the system to prove your injuries are real and documented," Fausone said, her frustration evident.

She has made it a personal mission to knock down barriers for veterans in these situations. In fact, she half-jokingly calls herself the "Chief Fix-It Officer" for veterans navigating red tape, quipping that "it shouldn't take a brigadier general to fix an issue for a vet, but it helps."[71] That wry remark speaks volumes. Too often, it has taken someone of her rank and tenacity to get a veteran's records transferred or benefits approved.

Progress is slowly being made. Fausone acknowledges initiatives such as the effort to create a single, integrated electronic health record for the DOD and the VA so that "the VA and DOD speak the same language" in healthcare. That project, launched in 2018, promises that one day, a service member's medical history will "follow them digitally from the battlefield to the VA clinic." But she is quick to note that "promises aren't enough, and veterans need continuity now."

Struggling for Care

Perhaps nowhere do the gaps in our current system show more painfully than in the ongoing struggle for access to appropriate care, especially for invisible injuries such as TBI. Curtis Armstrong's experience demonstrates both the high cost of those struggles and the hopeful possibilities when care is done right. I have known Armstrong for years now. He's not only a veteran of the Iraq War but also an

71 Chris Travers, "Campbell Native Makes Name for Herself at Veterans' Clinic," *Vindicator*, August 30, 2024, https://www.vindy.com/news/local-news/2024/08/campbell-native-makes-name-for-herself-at-veterans-clinic/.

ambassador with our Resurrecting Lives Foundation (RLF), dedicating himself to helping fellow vets with TBI. But his journey to healing was anything but straightforward.

Armstrong was injured during his 2006 deployment, exposed to multiple blast events that left him with classic post-concussion symptoms such as memory loss, splitting headaches, and trouble concentrating. Yet, when it was time for his Army exit physical, he was given only a cursory exam, according to his recollection.

"They asked if I was feeling OK, and I said, 'Well, I forget things, and my head hurts a lot,'" he recalls. "But since I could still walk and talk, they stamped my papers and said I was good to go."[72] The doctors did not connect the dots between his symptoms and a possible brain injury.[73] Again, records are key.

Like hundreds of thousands of others, his TBI went unrecognized at discharge—a hauntingly common occurrence in the 2000s when awareness was low and many in the military medical system weren't looking for brain wounds. "We can all imagine that if you're not looking for something, you won't find it," Curtis says with a bitter smile, echoing a hard truth.[74] In the years immediately after service, his undiagnosed TBI led to a cascade of problems.

He struggled in college because he couldn't remember what he'd studied. He had to write down simple tasks at work to compensate for cognitive lapses, which made him feel ashamed and "stupid," as he put it. Worst of all, his mood plummeted.

"I thought I was going crazy," he admits. Doctors outside the VA prescribed antidepressants, assuming he was just dealing with PTSD

72 Curtis Armstrong, interview by Chrisanne Gordon, *Guarding Our Guardians*.

73 Montgomery J. Granger, "Congress Reacts to Military Mental and Brain Health Issues," *Blaze*, May 7, 2014, https://www.theblaze.com/contributions/congress-reacts-to-military-mental-and-brain-health-issues-2.

74 Granger, "Congress Reacts to Military Mental and Brain Health Issues."

or readjustment. The VA, for its part, initially rated him for PTSD and hearing loss but did not include a diagnosis of TBI. "I kept telling them something wasn't right up here," he says, tapping his temple, "but I got more pills instead of real answers."

It wasn't until Armstrong connected with a TBI research advocate, through what would become the RLF, that he finally got a comprehensive neuro evaluation, including advanced imaging. Sure enough, a diffusion tensor imaging (DTI) scan (a special MRI technique that highlights microscopic brain damage) revealed the physical proof of his injury: patterns of torn neural pathways consistent with blast exposure.

"On one hand, it was devastating to see the damage on the scan," he told me. "But on the other hand, I wanted to frame it. It validated everything. I could finally say: This is not 'in my head' as a figure of speech. It's in my head as a real, medical fact."

That validation was the key that unlocked proper treatment. With a documented TBI diagnosis in hand, Curtis gained access to appropriate care: cognitive rehabilitation therapy, memory tools, headache clinics, and the camaraderie of other brain injury survivors. It transformed his trajectory. "It was like I'd been crawling through darkness, and someone finally handed me a flashlight," he said of getting into a TBI-focused rehab program.

Yet, for every Curtis Armstrong who eventually gets the right care, there are countless others still struggling. Armstrong often shares his story precisely to illustrate the critical importance of early diagnosis and continuity of care. "No one coming home with a brain injury should have to wander lost for years like I did," he insists.

His experience underscores several system failures we have discussed: the inadequate screening at the point of separation, the disconnect between DOD and VA records (his in-theater concussion reports never made it into his permanent file), and the historic tendency for the VA to over-rely on psychiatric medication in lieu of providing proper neurological rehab.

I asked Curtis what he wants policymakers and medical leaders to learn from his ordeal. His answer was direct: "Treat the injury, not just the symptoms. If I had a broken leg, they wouldn't just give me painkillers; they'd set the bone," he responded. "With TBI, they were handing me painkillers and antidepressants, but nobody was treating the actual injury to my brain until much later."

This aligns perfectly with what we, as advocates, have been shouting from the rooftops: TBI is now recognized as a physical injury to the brain often requiring targeted therapies, cognitive support, and ongoing holistic therapies. Armstrong also highlighted the need for persistence and advocacy.

"Honestly, if I hadn't met people who knew about TBI, I'd probably still be in the dark. Vets shouldn't need a Dr. Gordon to swoop in just to get proper care, but right now a lot of them do." His humility in calling me out aside, I know he's right. The system must evolve so that any veteran with a brain injury is immediately identified and guided into care, without needing a lucky encounter or the help of an external foundation.

Curtis Armstrong's journey, while painful, ultimately became a story of hope and purpose. With treatment, his cognitive function improved, his depression lifted, and he found new purpose in advocacy. He's now a TBI researcher himself, working on a public health degree and contributing to studies on veterans' brain health. "I went from being a statistic to helping change the statistics," he says proudly. By using his experience to educate lawmakers and clinicians, he's ensuring that what happened to him doesn't happen to the next generation.

The Needs of Women Guardians

While many challenges affect all of our Guardians, women veterans have unique healthcare needs and face additional hurdles that warrant special attention. This was a point that Brig. Gen. (Ret.) Carol Ann Fausone stressed in our conversation, and her perspective is bolstered by both the credibility of her rank and the insight of someone who has championed women's health within the VA system.

Women are the fastest-growing segment of the veteran population. Over the past forty years, the number of women in uniform has risen dramatically, with women now serving in virtually all roles, including combat duties.[75] "The service academies are enrolling women, more women are combat pilots and infantry leaders—we've proven ourselves in every sphere," Fausone noted, "but the system hasn't fully caught up to us once we hang up the uniform."

One glaring example she gives is the lack of a seamless continuum of care for gender-specific issues. For instance, a woman Army medic might receive excellent prenatal care on active duty, but upon transition to veteran status, she finds the local VA clinic has no OB-GYN on staff or long wait times for women's health appointments. "We have to ensure that when a woman warrior becomes a veteran, she doesn't lose access to the basic care she needs—whether that's gynecological care, breast cancer screenings, or mental health support attuned to women's experiences," Fausone told me.

Historically, VA medical centers were designed with male veterans in mind. Women often found themselves in clinics and waiting rooms full of men, sometimes feeling uncomfortable or invisible. "I've had female veterans tell me they were assumed to be a spouse or caregiver when they walked into a VA, because people didn't expect to see a

75 Travers, "Campbell Native Makes Name for Herself at Veterans' Clinic."

young woman veteran," she said. This kind of inadvertent bias can discourage women from seeking care. In fact, women veterans have utilized VA services at lower rates than men, partly because of these cultural and logistical barriers.

Telehealth and Tech

In the past decade, telehealth and wearable technology have emerged as promising tools to reach and treat post-9/11 veterans, especially those in remote areas or those dealing with mobility and mental health challenges. These innovations hold great promise, but as experts underscore, they also have their limitations and must be integrated thoughtfully into veterans' care.

Telehealth saw dramatic expansion in the VA, particularly driven by necessity as nearly half of post-9/11 vets live in rural areas. From her strategic vantage, Brig. Gen. (Ret.) Fausone lauds telehealth as "one of the best things to happen for veterans' access." She points out that for a vet living one hundred miles from the nearest VA hospital, a video appointment with a specialist can be life-changing.

"It's about bringing care to the veteran, instead of always bringing the veteran to the care," she says, echoing a new VA mantra. In her legal practice helping our Guardians, she has seen clients in rural Michigan get PTSD counseling or TBI follow-ups via secure video, where otherwise they might have skipped treatment because of travel barriers. Tele-mental health in particular, Fausone notes, has been a "godsend" for veterans who feel more at ease opening up from the comfort of home.

However, both Fausone and Armstrong caution that telehealth is not a panacea. "Technology is only as good as its connectivity," Fausone reminded me, highlighting the practical issue that many rural or underserved communities lack reliable broadband internet, which can turn a video session into a frustrating experience. The VA and Congress have been working on expanding broadband access and providing tablets to vets who need them, but the digital divide still leaves some behind.

Additionally, Fausone points out that certain types of care still require a hands-on approach: "You can't do a dental exam or a blood draw over Zoom. And when it comes to something like a neurological exam for TBI, there are parts you want to do in person." Her take-home message is that telehealth should augment, not replace, in-person care when needed. She also notes that some older veterans or those with cognitive impairments may struggle with the technology itself.

Wearable technology is another frontier that excites but warrants realistic expectations. We live in an age of smartwatches, fitness trackers, and health apps that can monitor everything from heart rate and sleep patterns to mood indicators. I've encountered Guardians who swear by their Apple Watch or Fitbit to help manage their post-combat life. For example, some use sleep trackers to detect undisturbed versus restless sleep, which can signal nightmares or anxiety.

Others use meditation apps that pair with heart rate sensors. When the device senses a rise in pulse and an increase in stress, it can prompt a breathing exercise. There are even emerging tools specifically designed for PTSD. In fact, in 2025, researchers at Texas A&M unveiled a smartwatch-based PTSD management system called First Watch Device.[76]

Armstrong has tried some of these gadgets, given his role as an RLF ambassador, always looking at new resources. He found a wearable that helped track his sleep and headaches. "I learned

76 Justin Kraiza, "New Wearable Tech Aims to Transform PTSD Care for Veterans and First Responders," *Fox San Antonio*, May 2, 2025, https://foxsanantonio.com/newsletter-daily/new-wearable-tech-aims-to-transform-ptsd-care-for-veterans-and-first-responders-texas-am-aggies-college-station-university.

that on days I was more stressed, my smartwatch showed I'd get almost no deep sleep. It kind of pushed me to take sleep hygiene seriously," he said.

He also tried a beta version of a stress-monitoring app that would vibrate to gently alert him when his physical signs of anxiety were creeping up. "Sometimes, I didn't even notice I was clenching my jaw or holding my breath, and then I'd feel the buzz and realize, oh, I need to calm down," he recalled. These self-management tools can empower veterans to understand and influence their own health in ways that were previously not possible.

Holistic and Integrated Care

Emerging from all these discussions is a vision of veteran healthcare that is holistic, tech-enabled, and fully integrated with civilian resources. This is not just a lofty ideal; it's a practical model already taking shape in pockets of innovation, and our expert voices strongly advocate for expanding these models.

Brig. Gen. (Ret.) Fausone, with her dual experience in military medicine and civilian healthcare advocacy, is a big proponent of integrative care models. "We need to treat the whole veteran—body, mind, and community," she told me. What does that mean in practice? For one, it means leveraging every tool available to diagnose and treat injuries like TBI and PTSD. Fausone is excited by the increasing use of advanced brain imaging (such as DTI and functional MRI) in the VA and research centers, which can reveal subtle brain changes that standard scans miss.

"For years, veterans were told 'nothing's wrong, your MRI is normal,' while they clearly were suffering. Now we can see the damage in many cases—tiny white matter lesions, disrupted neural pathways. It's validating and it guides treatment," she explained.

She also notes that biomarkers—whether from imaging, blood tests, or cognitive assessments—can help tailor therapies to the individual. This is the kind of precision medicine approach that modern technology allows, and she wants the VA to continue investing in it. It's not lost on her that her alma mater, the University of Michigan, has been at the forefront of some of these developments, and she's proud of the role veterans have played in pushing for better diagnostics.

Therapeutically, virtual reality (VR) therapy is something both Fausone and I have witnessed showing great promise. VR exposure therapy, for example, creates computer-generated environments to help veterans with PTSD confront and process traumatic memories in a controlled setting. The BraveMind program, developed with DOD funding, is one such VR system already used at several VA hospitals.[77] I have personally sat with Guardians as they donned VR headsets and virtually "returned" to a Baghdad street or an Afghan village, this time with a therapist guiding them through the triggered memories to reduce their power.

It's intense but effective, and studies show significant reductions in PTSD symptoms for those who undergo VR exposure therapy.[78] Technologies such as VR therapy could have accelerated Armstrong's diagnosis and treatment. Another aspect of holistic care is incorporating alternative and complementary therapies into mainstream treatment. This includes everything from mindfulness meditation, yoga, and art therapy to acupuncture for pain or equine therapy for emotional healing.

77 "Virtual Reality for In Vivo Exposure for Post Traumatic Stress," *VA Innovation Marketplace*, accessed July 14, 2025, https://marketplace.va.gov/innovations/bravemind.

78 "Virtual Reality Exposure Therapy (VRET)," *BrainLine*, March 2021, https://www.brainline.org/treatment-hub-treating-brain-injury-and-ptsd/virtual-reality-exposure-therapy-vret.

Both Fausone and Armstrong have seen veterans thrive when given access to these options. Armstrong, for instance, found unexpected relief through a simple mindfulness practice. "I learned to do meditation and deep breathing through a program you recommended," Armstrong told me. "I thought it was hocus pocus at first, but it ended up being one of the best tools for my anxiety and focus."

He even tried yoga at a veterans' retreat and admitted with a laugh that despite being the "least flexible guy in the room," it helped alleviate his back pain and improve his sleep. Fausone added that these approaches often succeed because they give veterans active roles in their own healing. "It's not just passive treatment where something is done to you. You are actively retraining your mind and body," she says.

The practical takeaway is that the VA and community programs should continue to expand access to such holistic modalities, not as fringe extras but as core parts of a veteran's care plan. The evidence is mounting that they work, especially in combination with conventional treatments.

Crucially, civilian-integrated care models and data-sharing platforms tie everything together. When a veteran needs specialized care, the model of sending them to a top-tier civilian partner hospital has proven its worth. Fausone believes this collaborative approach should extend further: "If the best orthopedic surgeon for a particular vet is at a private hospital, the system should enable that referral. If a local community clinic can do follow-ups closer to the veteran's home, we should loop them in."

The VA MISSION Act has already made community care more accessible, allowing veterans to use private providers at the VA's expense under certain conditions. The next step is making sure all these players—the VA, the newly designated DOW, private providers, and the veteran—are connected by modern data-sharing platforms. This might mean a nationwide health information exchange for veterans or simply ensuring that the new federal Electronic Health Record system under rollout is fully interoperable.

In lay terms: If a veteran from rural Idaho goes to a local ER for a crisis, that ER should be able to instantly see their military and VA medical history, and whatever care it provides should flow back into their VA record. Likewise, the veteran themselves should have access to their own data.

Curtis illustrated how important integration is with a personal anecdote: "When I finally got into a good rehab program, it was at a private hospital that partnered with the VA. They had all my records. My military file, my VA assessments, even notes from a civilian neuropsychologist I'd seen. For the first time, I didn't have to repeat my story from scratch. Every provider was on the same page."

That experience, he said, not only made care more efficient but made him feel truly cared for. "I wasn't just a number being shuffled between silos. I was a person with a whole team behind me." That's the model we should be seeking: veteran-centric care with a coordinated team of VA and civilian healthcare advisors and specialists as needed, including therapists, tech tools such as proven apps or VR, and community support groups, all working from the same playbook.

Validating the Problems, Building the Solutions

As I reflect on Carol Ann Fausone's decades of service or Curtis Armstrong's hard-won wisdom, I find a strong narrative thread of validation and hope. The problems identified earlier in this book aren't figments of imagination or isolated anecdotes; they are echoed by generals and enlisted alike, by clinicians and patients.

That validation is important. It tells every struggling veteran reading this that you are not alone, and you were not wrong about the flaws you encountered. And nestled in each of these hard truths is hope—because in each case, someone, somewhere has begun to solve it. The experts and practical solutions highlighted here form a bridge from our diagnosis of the issues to the prescription of remedies.

We know what the problems are, and we have a pretty good idea of what the solutions look like. The frustration and the opportunity lie in execution. Gen. (Ret.) Fausone said it well: "It's not rocket science; it's political and social will. We must care enough to do it." These conversations reinforced that sentiment.

There is a moral urgency, yes, but also a refreshing practicality in the ideas discussed. We're not talking about abstract or impossible dreams; we're talking about implementing warm handoffs, training programs, better data systems, proven therapies, and compassionate practices that treat our Guardians with respect and acceptance. Many of these solutions have been piloted successfully on small scales. The task ahead is about implementation, scaling up these successes, institutionalizing them, funding them, and holding our institutions accountable for delivering them.

> That's the model we should be seeking: veteran-centric care with a coordinated team of VA and civilian healthcare advisors and specialists as needed, including therapists, tech tools such as proven apps or VR, and community support groups, all working from the same playbook.

To do this, we'll need a strong sense of collaboration.

CHAPTER 6

ALL HANDS ON DECK

The death of Sgt. Zachary McBride in Iraq in 2008 highlighted the ongoing cost of war. His death changed many worlds that day, including my own. I had already begun to sense my calling after reading that 2007 newspaper article accusing returning troops of "malingering."

But it was the heartbreaking loss of Sgt. McBride, a bright young man who deferred college to serve after 9/11, that crystallized my mission. On that day, I dedicated myself to making a change for our returning Guardians. I understood in my bones that no single doctor, no lone government agency, no one of us, could tackle the challenges these Guardians face. It would take all of us working together—military and civilian, government and community, families and caregivers—to truly guard those who guarded us.

What followed was the birth of the RLF in 2012. In launching the RLF, I knew we had to rally the full force of civilian resources to repair and restore the invisible wounds of war. From day one, we set out to partner instead of going it alone.

Our foundation started advocating for veterans within their local communities by referring them to nearby hospitals and clinics for diagnostics and treatment and actively collaborating with other nonprofits to coordinate job training and career opportunities for vets during their recovery. Essentially, the RLF became a bridge connecting the often-siloed military and VA systems with civilian healthcare and community support.

VA and Civilian Healthcare as Partners

One of the most enduring truths in this journey is that neither the VA nor the private healthcare system can succeed fully in isolation. Each holds pieces of the puzzle. The VA offers a deep understanding of military injuries and a dedicated network of facilities; the civilian sector provides innovation, capacity, and a competitive drive for quality. When these forces collaborate, our Guardians benefit.

Beyond policy, we must promote a cultural shift among VA and civilian providers, viewing one another not as competitors or adversaries but as complements within a broader network. Yes, there is a healthy element of competition that can drive better care. The VA should feel the pressure to perform because veterans now have other options. In my early days volunteering at the VA, I was struck by how some facilities lacked the customer-service mindset common in private hospitals. There was a sense that veterans had nowhere else to go, which sometimes bred complacency.

By contrast, civilian hospitals compete to attract patients, often by providing more compassionate and convenient services, which are rewarded by better Press Ganey survey scores. Injecting that competitive spirit into veterans' care is not about picking winners or privatizing the whole system; it's about creating an incentive for every provider to strive for excellence. When the VA knows a vet can see a local doctor if wait times are too long or quality is subpar, it must up its game.

And when private hospitals step up to share the load, they must learn the unique needs of veterans, often consulting with VA experts. In this way, competition and symbiosis go hand in hand: Each system challenges the other to improve, and each learns from the other's strengths. Ultimately, the veteran stands to gain from this "best of both worlds" approach.

Nonprofits and Foundations Filling the Gaps

If government and healthcare institutions form the framework of our Guardians' care, the nonprofit world provides much of the heart and creativity. Organizations outside the federal system often have the agility to pilot new solutions and the personal touch to reach veterans one by one. I have been continually inspired by groups such as the Elizabeth Dole Foundation, founded by former Senator Elizabeth Dole after she became a caregiver to her wounded husband.

Dole quickly recognized a national need, as the countless spouses, parents, and friends who serve as caregivers to injured veterans were often unseen and unsupported. Rather than waiting for the VA to deal with this alone, her foundation partnered with the VA to change the culture of care. In 2019, the VA and the Elizabeth Dole Foundation launched the Campaign for Inclusive Care, a joint initiative to integrate caregivers into veterans' healthcare teams.[79]

This meant developing training for VA clinicians on working with family caregivers, creating tool kits to involve caregivers in treatment plans, and essentially saying: no more sidelining the spouse, mom, or dad who came with the veteran. They are *all* part of the team.

79 U.S. Department of Veterans Affairs, "VA Strengthens Caregiver Support Program," *VA News*, October 1, 2019, https://news.va.gov/66762/va-strengthens-caregiver-support-program/.

The very fact that VA leaders welcomed this collaboration signaled progress. A decade ago, an outside nonprofit advocating for the caregivers of veterans might have been unthinkable. Today, thanks to advocates like Senator Dole, the VA is beginning to see family not as interfering but as indispensable. And the results are tangible. Caregivers report feeling more respected and informed, and our Guardians feel less alone in navigating their recovery. In January 2024, the board unanimously endorsed former Secretary of the VA Robert "Bob" McDonald to be the board chair, thereby solidifying the joint VA/civilian healthcare efforts.

My own nonprofit has similarly leaned on partnerships to amplify impact. We knew from the start that if a veteran with TBI is struggling in, say, rural Ohio, the solution won't come solely from a distant central office in Washington. It comes from neighbors and networks: the local hospital willing to perform an MRI and share the results with a VA clinic; the state university that opens a slot in its cognitive therapy program; the community business that offers a job adapted to the vet's abilities; the volunteer who drives the vet to appointments. RLF has made it our philosophy to "coordinate, not duplicate."

If a quality service exists, we'd rather link a veteran to that service than create our own version. That's how, in 2015, we teamed up with Honda of America and several employers in central Ohio to address veteran employment. Together, we launched an "Invest in Vets" initiative aimed not just at hiring but also employing and training veterans, including those struggling with TBI. In addition, we collaborated with Bowling Green State University in western Ohio and the University of Akron in eastern Ohio to provide VA telehealth services on campus, thereby enabling veterans to seek healthcare services while on campus.

The telehealth partnership even earned support from the state's governor, who signed it into the Ohio budget, formalizing a pipeline for veterans' healthcare, education, and employment. That kind of public–private–nonprofit collaboration is a force multiplier. None of us alone could have created as many opportunities as we did together, with each partner bringing resources and clout. For us at RLF, it reinforced a powerful sense that large-scale change can start with a personal story and yet succeed through collective action.

Large-scale change can start with a personal story and yet succeed through collective action.

Consider another example: Staff Sgt. Brian Piercy, a U.S. Army hero who died in Afghanistan in 2010. He was one of eight young men from his California high school to make the ultimate sacrifice in our post-9/11 wars. Brian's sacrifice led to inspiration for a pilot program in transitioning into civilian life at his military base, the Eighty-Second Airborne Division home, Fort Bragg. That idea involved an employment and education program at Fort Bragg, designed to enable military members to begin lining up jobs and college courses before they retire from the uniform.

Brian's sacrifice inspired that pilot program, but making it a reality required the buy-in of Army base leadership, local employers, and educators. From tragedy to tangible reform, it happened because a diverse group of people—grieving families, military brass, nonprofits, and civic leaders—came together with determination to honor one life by bettering many others.

I never cease to be moved by how often this pattern repeats: A personal experience lights a spark, and collaboration fans it into a flame of change. Every nonprofit founder I know in the veterans' space, including myself, can point to a moment. Maybe it was the loss of a friend, a crisis in one patient, or a chance meeting with a struggling vet that ignited their cause. But we quickly learn that passion isn't enough; we need partners in government, academia, business, and community to execute solutions at scale.

Why Families and Communities Are the Frontline Allies

While institutions and organizations can set programs in motion, we must never overlook the people at the very ground level of a veteran's life: their families and local communities. Healing from the wounds of war is not a journey a veteran should ever walk alone. In fact, many of our Guardians will tell you that their first caregiver or counselor isn't a doctor at the VA; it's often their spouse, parent, sibling, or battle buddy.

These support networks are the unsung heroes assisting our Guardians through the red tape of obtaining healthcare and other services, often with little formal training or resources. That's why including them in the circle of care is practical and necessary. When a VA medical center trains its staff to communicate better with a veteran's wife about his PTSD triggers, that's smart healthcare. When a private employer offers flextime to a National Guard spouse who's juggling work and caring for an injured partner, it's strengthening the fabric of the workforce. Taking care of the people who protected our freedoms makes sense—now and in the future.

In recent years, communities across America have stepped up to formalize this kind of grassroots support. One inspiring initiative is the Mayor's Challenge to Prevent Suicide Among Service Members, Veterans, and their Families, a program jointly run by the VA and the Substance Abuse and Mental Health Services Administration. This challenge called on local leaders, such as mayors, county officials, and tribal leaders, to develop community-wide action plans to reduce veteran suicide. The response was overwhelming: Teams in twenty-four cities and regions joined the Mayor's Challenge, coming together with veteran organizations and health experts to share data, launch peer support networks, and plug gaps in crisis services.[80]

I had the chance to observe one of these city teams in action and was struck by the diversity in the room. At the table were VA clinicians, as well as city public health officers, police chiefs, clergy, university researchers, veteran spouses, and even veterans themselves, openly sharing their struggles. This was not about top-down edicts, but neighbors brainstorming with neighbors on how to save lives—perhaps by improving outreach at the local AMVETS hall, or training 911 operators to ask if a caller is a veteran, or organizing safe storage of firearms during mental health crises.

The exact strategies varied by city, but the unifying principle was the same: The community owns a piece of the solution. And when communities own something, they sustain it. Long after the federal spotlight moves on, those local coalitions continue to meet, adapt, and care for their own.

Another powerful example of community leadership is happening in Los Angeles, which has one of the largest concentrations of veterans—and, sadly, homeless veterans—in the country. In 2023, Los Angeles Mayor Karen Bass declared veteran homelessness a top emergency and forged a bold partnership with the VA, county agencies, and nonprofits to help vets get off the streets.[81] This initiative pooled city housing vouchers, VA case management, county housing programs, and charity outreach teams into one concerted effort.

80 Substance Abuse and Mental Health Services Administration, "Governor's and Mayor's Challenges to Prevent Suicide Among Service Members, Veterans, and Their Families," accessed July 22, 2025, https://www.samhsa.gov/technical-assistance/smvf/challenges.

81 "Mayor Bass Announces Partnership Between VA and City to Provide Resources to Unhoused Veterans," *MyNewsLA*, January 2, 2025, https://mynewsla.com/government/2025/01/02/la-city-more-resources-to-bring-more-unhoused-veterans-inside/.

By streamlining housing vouchers and adding on-the-ground staff, they've been able to move our Guardians from sidewalk tents into stable housing at an accelerated rate.[82] At a press briefing, Mayor Bass stood side by side with the VA secretary, a county supervisor, and the head of a local veteran nonprofit, all of them pledging, "We are all in this together." It was a stirring display of unified purpose. One Navy veteran at the event, a gentleman named Harold Hicks, shared how he had been sleeping in his car after falling on hard times.

Through this program, outreach workers found him, helped him secure a housing voucher, and paired him with a landlord willing to give a vet a chance. Hicks held up the key to his new apartment and addressed the crowd: "I want to encourage any veterans living on the streets to reach out and get help ... and I ask property owners to be part of this patriotic effort to house vets like me."[83] There were tears in more than a few eyes. In that moment, it was so clear: When a community decides that even one veteran living in despair is unacceptable, and everyone pulls in the same direction, miracles can happen.

Los Angeles still has a long way to go, but hundreds of veterans are already in permanent housing because of this all-hands effort. And tellingly, it was the collective voice of local leaders through the U.S. Conference of Mayors that helped change federal policy to support this cause, and they successfully lobbied to remove bureaucratic barriers that forced veterans to choose between housing assistance and disability benefits.[84] By working together and speaking up, they literally changed the rules to better honor those who served.

82 "Mayor Bass Announces Partnership Between VA and City to Provide Resources to Unhoused Veterans."

83 "Mayor Bass Announces Partnership Between VA and City to Provide Resources to Unhoused Veterans."

84 "Mayor Bass Announces Partnership Between VA and City to Provide Resources to Unhoused Veterans."

Accountability, Transparency, and a New Standard of Care

Collaboration is a powerful lever for accountability and transparency. Think about it: When multiple stakeholders are engaged in a veteran's welfare, it becomes much harder for systemic problems to hide in the shadows. In the words of Justice Brandeis, sunlight is a great disinfectant, and in the context of veterans' care, collaboration shines that light.

Perhaps the reason our Guardians struggled with opaque systems such as long waitlists, denied claims with little or no explanation, and health records lost in bureaucratic voids was that the VA operated in a silo. Now, when a city's mayor, a nonprofit, or a team of doctors from a university hospital is working with the VA on a common mission, there are external eyes on internal processes, and, more importantly, external hands to assist.

In my experience, VA administrators are very helpful when a respected outside partner is at the table advocating for a veteran. It's no longer an internal complaint that may get lost in red tape; it's a community concern that must be addressed in the open. In the wave of commitment from many new VA administrators, such as Mr. Glenn Costie, with whom I have worked, the strides toward collaboration and care are remarkably long and swift.

One idea gaining traction to cement this openness is the creation of a Veterans' Patient Bill of Rights. While the VA does publish a basic list of patient rights, including the right to respectful treatment and to be informed about care, many advocates feel that we need something more robust and specific to veterans' unique situation. I'm not talking about a symbolic pledge on a poster. I mean a codified set of guarantees that every veteran can count on and every provider (VA or otherwise) must uphold.

For instance, such a Bill of Rights could guarantee timely access to care, so that no veteran is ever left languishing for months for an appointment. It could ensure continuity of care and records, mandating that whenever a vet transitions from the DOW to the VA or from the VA to community care, their information and treatments transfer with them. No more starting from zero. It could enshrine the right to choose an outside provider if the VA can't deliver in a reasonable time or offer a needed specialty, effectively codifying the access standards from the MISSION Act so they can't be rolled back.[85]

It might affirm the inclusion of caregivers and family in care planning, recognizing them as partners in healing. And critically, it should spell out accountability measures: clear avenues for veterans to voice concerns or appeal decisions, as well as requirements for the VA to report outcomes and wait times transparently to the public.

As one veterans' advocate put it, "a veteran's bill of rights is needed so that veterans and VA staff know exactly what benefits veterans are entitled to."[86] In other words, clarity of expectations on both sides. Imagine if every transitioning service member were handed a plain-language document that said, "Here is what you have a right to expect from the VA and any partner providers. If you don't receive these things, here's who will fix it." That would be empowering.

It would also provide a checklist for Congress and communities to measure the VA's performance. Some lawmakers have even proposed legislation along these lines, seeking to codify MISSION Act policies and protect veterans' access to community care as a

85 Kristina Becvar, "Project 2025: The Department of Veterans Affairs," *Fulcrum*, July 5, 2024, https://thefulcrum.us/governance-legislation/project-2025-veterans.

86 Sharon Schlerf, "What Is Project 2025," *Veteran Pathways Home*, July 31, 2024, https://www.veteranpathwayshome.org/post/what-is-project-2025.

permanent right.[87] In my view, a Veterans' Patient Bill of Rights could become the North Star for collaboration: a common standard that the VA, private healthcare, and local supporters all commit to meeting.

Accountability must cut both ways. Just as we demand transparency and efficiency from institutions, we, as citizens, must hold ourselves accountable for how we treat those who have borne the battle. *Accountability* isn't just a bureaucratic term here. It's a moral one. It means ensuring that the promises made in glossy brochures or political speeches actually materialize in a veteran's day-to-day life.

Promises such as "You won't have to fight for your benefits," "We will support your brain health," or "Your family will be cared for too." Keeping these promises requires constant vigilance and collaboration. It might mean, for example, a state legislature stepping up to fill a gap that the federal system hasn't, as Ohio did when it funded our telehealth initiative.[88]

If the VA is struggling in an area, community partners can apply pressure or, better yet, offer alternatives and participate in solutions. If a private provider mistreats a veteran, the VA can intervene on the veteran's behalf. If a law or policy isn't working, veterans and families can team with legislators to reform it. Nobody gets a free pass to shirk their duty because everyone is watching and working together.

In a sense, we cultivate positive peer pressure. All parties know they're expected to deliver for our vets, and if they don't, someone else at the table will point it out or step in to help. This is not about finger-pointing; it's about shared responsibility. We all rise to the occasion because we're all in the fight for veterans' rights.

87 "SEC 3 Chap 20 VA Proj2025 Stop the Coup 2025" (PDF), Stop the Coup 2025, accessed July 22, 2025, https://static1.squarespace.com/static/6547d46ce0be13435001c0ad/t/6580b5c8b79bd44cda01c22e/1702933960468/SEC+3_Chap+20_VA_Proj2025_StopTheCoup2025.pdf.

88 "Our Story," Resurrecting Lives Foundation, accessed July 22, 2025, https://resurrectinglives.org/our-story.

Guarding the Guardians Together

Throughout this book, we've examined challenges that seem, at times, overwhelmingly complex: TBI that requires years of specialized care, potential crisis intervention, bureaucratic mazes, and transitions to civilian life fraught with pitfalls. It's easy to become disheartened by the scope of the problems. But here is what gives me hope every single day: Small groups of concerned people have made great progress in care provisions—in the VA, in the private sector, in non-profits, on Capitol Hill. And what more worthy cause could there be than keeping our nation's promise to its Guardians?

> Small groups of concerned people have made great progress in care provisions—in the VA, in the private sector, in nonprofits, on Capitol Hill.

I write these words as both a call to action and a promise grounded in experience. I have seen what happens when we marshal the power of partnership. I've seen an injured veteran go from despair to hope because a VA counselor, a nonprofit caseworker, and a devoted wife put their heads together and crafted a support plan as a unit. I've watched formerly skeptical VA officials become champions of change after sitting down with veterans and caregivers in town halls, listening to their truths in a collaborative spirit. I've stood in awe as a small group of regular citizens changed the world for a veteran. From the local volunteers in our comedy therapy groups to the top brass, such as Gen. (Ret.) Fausone, who knock down bureaucratic barriers, each has proven that no contribution is too small when aligned with a greater good.

Make no mistake, this is not about creating some new massive bureaucracy or passing the buck. It's about leveraging the strengths of each player: the VA's capacity and expertise, the private sector's innovation and speed, nonprofits' passion and personalization, families' intimate knowledge and commitment, and communities' vigilance and unity. It's about fostering a culture where transparency is expected, help is welcomed from all quarters, and pride is taken not in who gets credit but in the outcomes for our Guardians. In such a culture, even healthy competition serves a greater purpose because everyone's eye is on the same prize: better care and better lives for those who served. We have been the beneficiaries of our veterans' past protection of our freedom. Now, we owe them a future.

Looking forward, I envision a day when the phrase "veterans' healthcare reform" is no longer necessary in our vocabulary because it will simply be how we do business as a nation. A day when a young Marine recovering from a brain injury seamlessly moves from a military clinic to a VA hospital to a private rehab center near his hometown, without a glitch or gap in treatment—because all those entities operate as one collaborative network. A day when every veteran and family member can recite their fundamental rights in the care system, and those rights are consistently met, not as lofty ideals but as everyday practice.

This future is within reach. As I write this, many of these ideas are already being piloted on small scales with success. The task ahead is scaling up these successes, institutionalizing them, and holding ourselves accountable for delivering them. It comes down to what Gen. (Ret.) Fausone told me, her voice ringing with common sense: "It's not rocket science, it's political and social will. We have to care enough to do it."

Collaboration is not a spectator sport. Whether you're a medical professional, a business owner, a public official, a neighbor, or simply a citizen who cares, you have a role to play. It can be as grand as forming a public–private coalition to tackle veteran homelessness, or as personal as offering to babysit for an exhausted caregiver down the street. It all counts.

Years ago, I began this journey outraged by an article and heartbroken by the loss of a young veteran I never got to meet. I felt in my gut that we could do better. Today, having witnessed incredible transformations born of collaboration, I know in my heart that we *are* doing better and that we will do better still, as long as we keep working together.

SECTION III

EDUCATION

CHAPTER 7

FROM COMBAT BOOTS TO TEXTBOOKS

When I turned my attention from battlefield injuries to the battlefield of higher education, I discovered a maze of challenges that our Guardians must navigate.

In theory, programs such as the GI Bill should make attending college or technical training simple. In practice, the path is littered with confusing rules, bureaucratic snares, and cultural landmines that can derail even the most determined veteran. I learned this through both research and the personal stories veterans shared with me.

One veteran in particular, Matt Garrett, opened my eyes to just how convoluted and treacherous this journey can be. Garrett served as a Navy corpsman with the U.S. Marines and completed two combat tours of duty. The first was with the initial wave in 2003, and then he went back again in the summer of 2005, returning home in April 2006. After over five years of active duty, he received his honorable discharge. His story, along with others, highlights why we must fundamentally rethink how we guide our Guardians from the military into the classroom.

The GI Bill has long been regarded as a golden ticket and a way for those who serve to get a college education or job training afterward. I certainly viewed it that way, assuming it was a straightforward benefit. But as I dug in, I found no less than *four* different versions of the GI Bill, each with its own eligibility rules and quirks.

There's the Montgomery GI Bill for active duty, a separate Montgomery GI Bill for the Selected Reserve, a program for dependents of disabled veterans, and the Post-9/11 GI Bill. Keeping them all straight is a challenge even for the experts. One of the first hurdles comes at the very start of a military career, often in boot camp.

Garrett, a Navy corpsman, described an almost hard-to-believe scene on day one of boot camp. Amid the whirlwind of becoming a recruit, a drill instructor asked him and his peers point-blank, "Do you want the GI Bill or not?" This came with the catch that if you do, the military will dock $100 from your pay each month during that first year. In 2003, a newly enlisted Navy recruit at the E-1 (Seaman Recruit) level received $1,064.70 in basic monthly pay for their first four months of service. Once they completed this initial period, their monthly pay increased to $1,150.80.

Garrett was eighteen years old, earning maybe $20,000 a year in those early ranks, and he was being told that to secure future education benefits, he had to give up a chunk of his meager pay. "Did you know that?" he asked me later. "I didn't know that." I was stunned. I'd never heard of this myself, and I've been working with our Guardians for years.

It turns out this policy was part of the old Montgomery GI Bill. Service members paid $100 per month to be eligible, and even if that money is ultimately a good investment in one's future, for a teenager fresh out of high school, it felt like a shakedown. Pay now, or you'll never get your education benefit.

And in fact, the choice was presented as irrevocable. Garrett recalls being warned emphatically that if he said "no" in that moment, he could never sign up for the GI Bill later. A one-time, now-or-never decision, made under pressure, on literally his first day in uniform. It blew my mind hearing this. Who on earth designs a benefit for veterans that way?

It felt like a trap laid for the young and uninformed, and it clearly bothered Garrett (and me) that the system would operate in such a manner. As he put it, it felt as if they were "trying to manipulate young minds who are just trying to do the right thing," boxing them into a lifetime decision about education before they've even finished basic training."

To the DOD, this policy may have made financial sense at one time, perhaps to ensure only those serious about using the benefit would opt in, thereby saving money. But from where I sit now, it's indefensible. We don't ask eighteen-year-olds in any other walk of life to predict whether they'll want a college education five, ten, or twenty years down the line.

Why did we think newly enlisted soldiers and sailors could do that? In recent years, thankfully, this $1,200 buy-in for the Post-9/11 GI Bill has been eliminated. Yet, many of our Guardians who served under the older rules, like Matt Garrett, are still navigating the ripple effects of that policy today.

Countdown Clocks and Confusing Deadlines

Even after a veteran does secure their GI Bill entitlement, the challenges are far from over. One big issue is timing. Many Guardians don't transition straight from active duty to college, nor should we expect them to. After years of war or intensive service, a person might need time to heal, work through health issues, or simply readjust to civilian life before plunging into an academic program.

Unfortunately, the GI Bill historically came with expiration dates that often failed to account for these realities. Garrett discovered this the hard way. He had assumed, as many do, that his education benefits would be there whenever he was ready. In theory, the VA made it sound like you could use your GI Bill at your own pace, up to a certain credit cap. In practice, hidden deadlines lurked beneath the fine print.

For the Montgomery GI Bill, you used to have ten years from your last discharge to use the benefit or lose it. Garrett left the service in the mid-2000s, so that ten-year clock was ticking down on him. Worse, he told me he found out that once he started using his GI Bill, another shorter clock started, about seven years to finish using it up, or he'd lose the remainder.

Imagine the pressure that creates. You not only have to decide when to start school, but once you do, you can't take too long to complete your degree or use up all your benefits, even if life intervenes. As Garrett put it, "some of [the benefits] are written for seven years only, some for ten, but at the end of that, that's a cutoff."

He had no idea about this when he enlisted or even when he first enrolled in college. It was a nasty surprise that he described as "mind-boggling" once he learned of it. And he wasn't alone; even those of us trying to research the latest rules find them perplexing, since Congress has updated the laws repeatedly.

For example, the 2017 "Forever GI Bill" finally eliminated the fifteen-year expiration on the Post-9/11 GI Bill, but only for veterans discharged during or after 2013. Those who got out earlier (like many Iraq/Afghanistan vets) still faced deadlines. The patchwork of rules is dizzying. Garrett noted that even VA representatives and veteran program staff can get it wrong or be out of date on these details. When he and I talked, neither he nor another seasoned veterans' advocate we know (Don Accamando—more on his visionary program later) was fully aware of the latest changes. That's how rapidly the rules keep shifting.

Consider what these ticking clocks meant for someone like Garrett. He came home from two combat deployments with physical and psychological wounds, and even lost his mother, his singular rock and parent, to cancer not long after. At twenty-seven, he found himself adrift as a single male with no kids.

Most of his friends were already working and building their lives, while he was grieving, healing, and trying to rediscover his purpose after the military. In that state, he wasn't ready to dive into college immediately, or he struggled to stay in school consistently. But the GI Bill's timers don't care about personal circumstances.

"Even if I don't start [school right away], I still have to finish [using the benefit] in ten years," he explained with frustration. The pressure to use it or lose it only added to his stress at a vulnerable time. In fact, he nearly *did* lose it. He recounted taking time off to focus on his mental health, going to an agricultural therapy program to heal, and then realizing that the clock was still winding down.

"I was really battling hard. Not even just for school, but for my life," he said. He mentioned that on certain days, he was unsure he would be on this earth the next. "What's my purpose now?" he told me. Hearing that our system broke his warrior spirit totally broke my heart. A veteran who had already sacrificed so much was put in the position of racing a bureaucratic deadline to save an education benefit that he rightfully earned, all while he was literally fighting to stay alive and find meaning after war. Our Guardians should not have these battles when they return.

It's no wonder he ended up needing a counselor's intervention, and thankfully, that intervention was in time. Garrett recalls a university counselor urging him to stop comparing himself to his civilian peers and recognizing that "most people wouldn't be [here]" if they had been through what he had. In other words, most people in his situation might not even be alive, let alone trying to finish college.

Thankfully, with support, Garrett did persevere and ultimately graduated in late 2011 with a bachelor's degree in history. But it was a close call on multiple levels. How many other vets have we lost along the way because of these arbitrary limits? How many gave up on school—or worse, gave up completely—because the system piled on pressure instead of providing patience and support?

In addition, Garrett was a highly trained and highly skilled Navy Corpsman whose ability to care for individuals in medical crisis is unsurpassed in our nation. Why did he never receive counseling about how close he was to a degree in healthcare? He loved what he was doing in the Navy. He excelled academically, earning high honors throughout his training. So, why wasn't he encouraged to pursue a pathway to success, rather than struggling to find the right degree in a timely manner for the GI Bill?

There have been improvements. The Forever GI Bill (named as such because it removed that expiration for newer vets) was a step in the right direction. But for many veterans, those changes came too late to help them. And even now, not every restriction is gone; other programs, such as certain job training benefits or Vocational Rehabilitation, have their own sets of rules and timelines.

The big picture is this: Educational benefits should be available to be utilized as the recovery timeline and needs of the veteran allow. Otherwise, we're giving with one hand and taking away with the other.

When Benefits Stall and Bills Come Due

Even after a veteran manages to enroll in school using the GI Bill, another common challenge rears its head: cash flow. The Post-9/11 GI Bill, for instance, covers tuition directly to the school and provides a monthly housing allowance to the student. It sounds straightforward, but in practice, I've heard repeated accounts of delays in payments that cause serious hardship.

Garrett experienced this as well. After enrolling for classes one fall, he waited month after month for his first housing stipend to arrive. "You sign up for school in September, but your first payment doesn't come for months," he told me. In his case, the first GI Bill payment didn't show up until February of the next year. That's nearly five months with no support, even though he was a full-time student, presumably unable to work much on the side.

Now, imagine being in that situation. You've left a steady military paycheck and jumped into school, trusting that the promised benefits will sustain you. Rent is due, groceries need to be bought, maybe you have a family to feed, and the money is just not there.

Unless you have savings or family to lean on, you're in trouble. "What am I supposed to do?" Garrett asked pointedly when relating this memory.

Any of those options can derail a veteran's education before it even begins. Remember, they are already significantly behind those who graduated from high school with them. This kind of delay is often due to administrative backlog. The VA processing can be slow, especially if there are any paperwork hiccups between the school certifying your enrollment and the VA cutting the check.

But from the veteran's vantage point, the reason matters little when you're scraping together rent. The GI Bill housing allowance is intended to replace the Basic Allowance for Housing that active-duty service members receive, recognizing that students still have living costs. Yet if it arrives a semester late, it might as well not be there at all.

It's an unacceptable failure of execution. The benefits need to be timely, just as paychecks were in the service. I can't help but think of how the military prides itself on logistics and reliability. We would never let combat troops go five months without their pay or their supplies; the system would move heaven and earth to fix it.

Why, then, do we allow our Guardians on campus to flounder for months while waiting for their benefits? If we truly value their transition, this is a nuts-and-bolts problem that should be eminently solvable. Faster processing, advance payments, and emergency bridge loans are all ways to prevent this hardship, and we owe it to our vets to implement them.

A Cultural Gulf in the Classroom

Even if all the GI Bill red tape were cut away, Guardians would still face another significant barrier in higher education: the cultural disconnect. Military service isn't just a job; it's an all-encompassing lifestyle that forges a unique identity. Stepping onto a college campus after years in uniform can feel like landing on a different planet.

I've seen it time and again. Young vets sitting in college classrooms or starting entry-level jobs, surrounded by peers whose biggest worry is that their Starbucks latte was cold, while the vet is thinking about buddies who almost died or friends still struggling just to, as one veteran told me, "keep on this side of the grass."

This cultural gulf breeds isolation. The veteran often feels they can't relate to the trivial day-to-day complaints of their classmates, and their classmates can't possibly relate to the veteran's life-and-death experiences. The more combat exposure or trauma a veteran has, the harder this adjustment becomes.

I will never forget one of the most chilling phone calls of my career, which underscored this problem. Around a decade ago, on a Saturday night, I received a cold call from a young man who had gotten my cell phone number from a previous caller, a phenomenon I call "the military/veteran hotline"—passed on from one vet to another.

This phenomenon has introduced me to some of the most remarkable warrior spirits on the planet. Although our foundation is *not* a suicide crisis line, we align heavily with our VA and national suicide hotlines, but this call was long before they were formed.

This veteran was a new freshman at an Ivy League East Coast school, and he was in absolute distress. Over the phone, his voice was shaking, and his words tumbled out rapid-fire. "I can't do this. I can't do this," he kept saying. He described sitting in basic English classes, feeling completely lost.

"The first day I was lost ... They all have these AP credits; they know how to write. I don't know any of this," he confessed. "I was in over my head from day one."

In high school, this young man had been the star football player, but academically, he'd been near the bottom of his small rural high school class, nowhere near the preparation level of a typical Ivy League student. His exceptional physical prowess and leadership skills on the playing field had served him and our nation well on the battlefield. Yet he was unprepared for the special veterans' program he had been recruited to. He was already four years out of high school, and his former "classroom" had been riddled with bombs, explosions, and tests of survival that the college campus could not imagine. During these bomb blasts, he had sustained brain injuries that had not yet healed and were impeding his learning processes.

Now he was in the Northeast megalopolis, surrounded by wealthy nineteen-year-olds, and he felt completely out of place. The impostor syndrome, the academic gaps, and the social isolation had all combined into a crisis. On that call, he revealed something that made me literally stop breathing. That Saturday night, he was sitting in his dorm closet with a gun, locked and loaded, contemplating whether to end his life. He had spiraled that far in just the first few weeks.

I remember my throat tightening with fear as I realized what he was implying. I kept him talking while simultaneously urging him to tell me his exact location and whether anyone else was around. His roommate was out at a party, he said. I gently but firmly instructed this desperate young man to call someone into the room—immediately. "Is there someone you can call? Where's your resident assistant or someone in your hall?"

Eventually, I got him to agree that his roommate's absence was dangerous and that we needed another person there. I stayed on the phone with him for what felt like a twelve-hour shift in the ER, but was, in fact, more like an hour—until, by a stroke of luck, that roommate returned to the dorm room. I spoke with the roommate, an understandably shocked and shaken nineteen-year-old, and coached him on what to do. "Call the VA suicide hotline and follow instructions." I remained with them while this was accomplished, and they received instructions.

"Stay with him tonight," the phone counselor and I urged. "Don't go back out to the party. Just be there. Pretend you're studying or watching TV, whatever, but don't leave him alone." Then he called in the resident assistant, who arrived to help.

Later that weekend, we talked the veteran through his immediate options. He could withdraw from the class or even the semester without penalty and take time to regroup. The Ivy League would still be there later if he wanted to return, but there was no shame in stepping back.

In the end, that's what he did. He dropped out, at least for the time being, and it likely saved his life, as did his roommate and his university counselors, who truly were navigating this GI Bill along with him. No one had anticipated the swift downward spiral, for TBI was not yet accepted as the signature wound of the GWOT, and our veteran had nearly become another suicide statistic attributed to untreated or undiagnosed TBI.

This was an extreme case, but I fear it is not as isolated as we'd like to think. Inviting a veteran to a highly competitive, elite university without any transitional support is a difficult hill to climb, no matter how well-meaning the university is or how attractive it is for the veteran. Our vets are coming straight from a tight-knit military environment, where collaboration is superior to competition; a much different environment and skill set than those at a competitive university campus.

In this instance, it almost ended in tragedy. And what haunted me was the realization that it all could have been avoided. Upon leaving the service, he might have been steered to a more suitable starting point. Say, a year at a community college near home to build up his academic skills, rather than leaping straight into the Ivy League deep end.

It's not that student veterans can't handle top-tier academics. Many absolutely can, but it has to be the right fit; it has to be at the right time—when brain injury has been treated and has improved.

Matching Our Guardians to the Right Educational Environment

This true story had a mercifully safe ending. The young man lived, and later he found another path that suited him better. But it was a wake-up call for me. It underscored the need for proactive guidance and realistic matching of Guardians to educational paths.

We must guard our Guardians from stumbling into an ambush in academia just as we would on the battlefield. In the military, we would never send a soldier on a mission without proper preparation, backup, and intel. Yet we routinely send veterans into any random college with nothing more than a pamphlet from the TAP. That has to change.

What might a better system look like? First, I believe every service member nearing discharge should receive personalized education counseling, just as they receive a briefing on healthcare and VA hospitals. In fact, during military out-processing, they often ask, "Where are you going to live? Here's how to enroll in VA healthcare there." We need an equivalent for education: "Where will you be moving to, and what schools or training programs are in that area? What do you want to study or do for a career? Let's map out a plan."

Right now, I see very little of that happening on a routine basis. Instead, it's left to the veteran to figure out later. That's backward. Not every veteran should immediately jump into a four-year university, and not every veteran should avoid it either. The key is matching the person to the right environment.

What are their academic strengths and weaknesses? What career are they aiming for? Do they thrive in smaller, hands-on settings or large lecture halls? These are questions that can be answered through aptitude tests, counseling interviews, and careful consideration of the veteran's background, as my colleague, U.S. Air Force veteran and Doctor of Education, Lt. Col. (Ret.) Don Accamando has emphasized.

The military has no shortage of aptitude tests. We test people when they join, and we test for specific skills. Why not test on the way out to help point them toward a fitting education/career track?

Dr. Accamando knew that there was immense value in peer mentorship and veteran-specific orientation. In the story above, one thing that could have helped is if the Ivy League program had assigned an upperclassman student veteran to mentor each incoming veteran, someone who had "been there" and could show the ropes and notice early if a fellow veteran was struggling. It brings to mind the old story from *The West Wing* about the parable of the man in a hole that Don Accamando likes to recount.

> This guy's walking down a street when he falls in the hole. The walls are so steep he can't get out. A doctor passes by, and the guy shouts up, "Hey, you, can you help me out?" The doctor writes a prescription, throws it down in the hole, and moves on. Then a priest comes along and the guy shouts up, "Father, I'm down in this hole. Can you help me out?" The priest writes out a prayer, tosses it down in the hole, and moves on. Then a friend walks by. "Hey Joe, it's me. Can you help me out?" And the friend jumps into the hole. Our guy says, "Are you stupid? Now we're both down here!" The friend says, "Yeah, but I've been down here before and I know the way out."[89]

One Size Will Not Fit All

I also learned about successful models from folks like U.S. Air Force Col. (Ret.) Mike Carrell at The Ohio State University (OSU). Not long after the Ivy League incident, OSU recognized this issue and, under Carrell's leadership, created a comprehensive office of military and veteran services. Within a few years, OSU went from having virtually nothing in place to becoming one of the leading veteran-friendly campuses.

Like fellow Air Force veteran Don Accamando, Carrell essentially built an entire support ecosystem so that what happened to our displaced veteran would never happen at OSU. This included orientation programs for veterans, academic tutoring, a veterans' lounge for peer connection, and trained staff who understood military culture. The results were immediately apparent. Fewer vets falling through the cracks, more vets graduating successfully. Many large universities followed suit, establishing veterans' centers and hiring coordinators to

89 John Spencer as Leo McGarry, in *The West Wing: Noël*, "The West Wing—Noël—Down in a Hole," YouTube video, 1:24, uploaded by Colin Barnette, published April 1, 2012, https://www.youtube.com/watch?v=VM56KXM4y4c.

focus on their needs. It has "gotten a lot better," I assure veterans now, compared to the bad old days when none of these supports existed.

Still, plenty of schools remain behind the curve. Many campus veterans' offices are understaffed and under-resourced, often just one well-meaning person trying to handle everything.[90] At schools without a strong veterans' program, student veterans can feel "camouflaged on campus," present but invisible, not identified or reached out to by anyone.[91]

I've heard Guardians say they don't even tell people they served because of the awkward or misinformed responses they get. One student veteran recounted how he stopped telling classmates or professors about his service because the minute he did, he'd hear things like, "Oh, you make me uncomfortable," or he'd be stereotyped as some angry vet.[92]

We also can't forget the experience of female Guardians. People often assume they're just spouses or dependents, not service members, which is another layer of disrespect that pushes them into silence.[93] All of this tells me that campus culture still needs work. Universities have to actively cultivate an environment where Guardians are valued and understood, not seen as outsiders who "talk funny" or as potential problems. This might involve training faculty on military culture, establishing visible veteran student clubs, or simply ensuring that someone checks in on veterans throughout the semester.

---

90 Diamond Smith et al., "Ohio Air Force Vet Helps Universities Serve Military Students Better," *WYSO*, June 26, 2025, https://www.wyso.org/military-aviation-news/2025-06-26/ohio-air-force-vet-helps-universities-serve-military-students-better.

91 Smith et al., "Ohio Air Force Vet Helps Universities Serve Military Students Better."

92 Smith et al., "Ohio Air Force Vet Helps Universities Serve Military Students Better."

93 Smith et al., "Ohio Air Force Vet Helps Universities Serve Military Students Better."

A particularly effective approach I've seen is steering veterans toward schools or programs that have a critical mass of other veterans and a track record of support. Community colleges and public universities in military-heavy regions tend to have a higher proportion of veterans, whereas some elite private colleges may have fewer veterans. "About 4.8 percent of students at community colleges are veterans, and approximately 1.6 percent are students on active duty or in the reserves/National Guard."[94]

For example, several young vets I met chose to start at Columbus State Community College in Ohio, specifically because it had a reputation for being vet-friendly. At that school, a retired Marine ran the veterans program, and he proactively grouped veterans in certain classes and majors so they wouldn't be isolated. He also assessed each vet's strengths and interests to "put people in [courses or programs] where they would succeed," essentially acting as an education coach, one of the many skills he developed while negotiating with tribal leaders in the GWOT. The difference was striking. Those vets thrived, built confidence, and many went on to transfer to four-year degrees or land good jobs.

They achieved success early on, which is really important. It's much better for a veteran to start at a level where they can excel and then ramp up, rather than be thrown into an environment where they're set up to fail from the start. This approach ought to be standard practice.

As we consider all these aspects—the financial hurdles, the bureaucratic nonsense, the cultural mismatch—one theme shines through: We need to be far more intentional about guiding our Guardians into and through higher education. After all, their high school counterparts

94 Timothy Prestianni, "71 Military and Veteran Higher Education Statistics for 2025," National University, November 29, 2024, https://www.nu.edu/blog/military-and-veteran-higher-education-statistics/.

who enter college after graduation have all the benefits of the school counselors and teachers.

Why shouldn't our Guardians have the same assistance, or better assistance, considering how different life in the military is compared to civilian life, especially in the large metropolitan areas? It's not enough to hand someone a benefits certificate and say, "Good luck at college." These men and women have been out serving their country, often in life-and-death situations, and many haven't written an essay or sat in a classroom since high school.

They've changed, and the world around them has changed. They've gained priceless survival and negotiating skills. They've learned to work as a team when the stakes are literally life or death. They left the twenty-first century for a year and returned in a day. To bridge that gap requires active measures.

At a minimum, I believe every transitioning service member should leave with an education plan in addition to a healthcare plan. This plan should consider their goals, abilities, family situation, and even mental health needs. If a vet has TBI or PTSD, for instance, maybe online courses or a lighter course load initially would be prudent, and that should be built into the plan.

If a vet comes from a rural area with a small local college, starting there or in a trade program might be a better option than immediately uprooting to a big city university. One size will not fit all; in fact, one size fits very few. As one study eloquently put it, current transition programs are too much of a "blanket" when in reality, "transition is such an individual process." We have to tailor our approach. Otherwise, we're going to keep seeing Guardians "unprepared, confused, and dispirited" by the abrupt drop-off in support when they enter civilian student life.

The problems are stark, but I remain hopeful because solutions are within reach. I've already witnessed pioneers developing those solutions—people who are finding ways to better serve those who served us. The stakes are high. Our Guardians' futures, and by extension, the future strength of our communities and nation, depend on us getting this right.

CHAPTER 8

EDUCATING THE EDUCATORS

Col. (Ret.) Mike Carrell has developed innovative approaches to veteran education support. Carrell is working at the National Veterans Leadership Foundation and has spent over a decade at OSU as an assistant vice provost in charge of the Office of Military and Veterans Services, and his work there became a model for universities nationwide. I was fortunate to speak with Carrell and to delve into some of his current efforts. What I learned from him is equal parts inspiring and sobering: inspiring because he's shown how much of a difference one dedicated office can make; sobering because so many places are still far behind where they need to be.

Carrell likes to point out that universities often simply don't know what they don't know when it comes to serving military students. He told me that he now often works directly with college presidents, provosts, and even boards of trustees, helping them create systemic changes on campus. "Our customers are the universities, not necessarily the military-connected students," he explained, "but everything we're trying to do is to improve [the universities'] programs, policies, and processes ... to give [those] students a better experience."[95] In

95 Smith et al., "Ohio Air Force Vet Helps Universities Serve Military Students Better."

other words, rather than trying to fix each veteran individually, Carrell focuses on fixing the institution.

He noted that most campus veteran offices in the United States are woefully understaffed, often just a single person or a small team tasked with handling everything from recruitment to advising to VA paperwork.[96] Some colleges didn't even have a dedicated staffer at all until recent years, and veterans' needs were scattered among various departments. Imagine being a twenty-two-year-old vet with TBI, trying to navigate admissions, financial aid, class registration, and counseling, and finding no single point of contact who understands your background.

It's easy to fall through the cracks in that scenario, and we've heard firsthand from our Guardians how devastating failure can be at this juncture in their careers. Carrell's work has been about convincing universities to invest in a one-stop veterans center, a place where a vet can go and be either helped directly or guided to the right service by people who "get it." One concept Carrell introduced me to is that of veterans being "camouflaged on campus." He means that in two senses.

First, student veterans don't necessarily stand out visibly. They might be older than the typical student, have a military haircut, or have a different demeanor, but often they try to blend in. Many won't voluntarily speak up about their service because they fear awkward reactions or stigmas. Most importantly, it seems, they want to avoid the most inappropriate, intrusive questions often rattled off lyrically by younger students, like "What is it like to kill someone?"

Second, administrators may not see the veterans unless they actively look. A vet might be struggling in silence, and a professor or administrator who's not attuned might just think, "Well, John hasn't been in class, guess he's slacking," whereas someone like Carrell

96 Smith et al., "Ohio Air Force Vet Helps Universities Serve Military Students Better."

would know that John is a vet and instead reach out to see if he needs support. Better yet, Col. (Ret.) Carrell doesn't ask. He just provides support, anticipating the needs of those he continues to serve.

Carrell stressed that data is key and universities should track how many vets they have, how those vets are doing, and survey their needs. It sounds basic, but many schools weren't even doing that until some enlightened universities and colleges began to employ former military members like Carrell to bridge the civilian and military gap and develop the necessary systems for success.

Carrell's own program at OSU became robust. They introduced orientation sessions specifically for our Guardians, pairing them with other student-vets. They had career fairs with veteran-friendly employers, mental health resources attuned to veterans, and even initiatives to make the campus bureaucracy easier for vets to navigate.

The payoff was significant: higher graduation rates for vets and a reputation that attracted more military-affiliated students to OSU. In fact, part of Carrell's job became advising other colleges on how to replicate that success. After retiring from OSU, he took on a national role, consulting with universities across the country to expand their support for the nearly one million student Guardians enrolled in higher education.

What I love about Carrell is that he couples realism with optimism. He doesn't sugarcoat the challenges. He freely admits, for example, that some faculty or staff do hold uninformed biases, like assuming every veteran has PTSD and is a potential "problem" in class. He's heard veterans say they feel either pitied or feared on campus, neither of which is conducive to learning.

But Carrell also sees the positive ripple effects when a campus gets it right. He shared that student veterans, when supported, tend to become campus leaders and community assets. They volunteer at higher rates and often take on mentorship roles for other students.[97] They bring diversity of experience and perspective to classroom discussions. And when they graduate, they continue that service mindset in their neighborhoods and companies.

"I know it sounds corny," Carrell told an interviewer, "But [these veterans are] going to change their little space at least. And by changing those spaces, we're going to change our state, country, and world."[98] If anything, military qualities, combined with higher education, can and should become a powerful force for good in society.

Carrell's point, and I echo it, is that investing in veterans' education yields dividends far beyond the individual. We're essentially cultivating a cohort of leaders and doers who have already proven their dedication. From Carrell's expert perspective, echoed by Dr. Accamando's program at Duquesne University, a few concrete recommendations emerge for any educational institution:

- First, establish a centralized veterans office with adequate staffing.
- Second, train the staff and willing faculty in military cultural competency.
- Third, track and proactively engage your student veterans.
- Fourth, create peer networks such as student veteran clubs or peer mentorship programs.
- Fifth, secure buy-in from top leadership that serving this population is a priority.

97 Smith et al., "Ohio Air Force Vet Helps Universities Serve Military Students Better."

98 Smith et al., "Ohio Air Force Vet Helps Universities Serve Military Students Better."

Carrell often notes that when university leadership is on board, things happen. If leadership is indifferent, even a passionate lower-level coordinator will struggle to make lasting changes. Thus, he spends a lot of time educating the educators, so to speak. Hearing from him reinforced my belief that every college president in America should be thinking about this. It's not just a "nice to have," it's part of their mission to educate and to serve the community.

Carrell also highlighted some less obvious aspects of veteran-friendly campuses. For instance, having a physical space, such as a veterans' lounge, can be important. It gives vets a place to find each other and decompress. But he warns that a lounge alone isn't enough, and you also need programming that integrates our Guardians into the broader campus life. The goal isn't to segregate vets, but rather to give them a springboard from which to fully participate in college.

Another point is credit for prior learning. Carrell pushed OSU and the state of Ohio to grant academic credit for some military training and experience. For example, an infantry squad leader might get leadership or physical education credits, while a medic might get health science credits. This not only acknowledges the learning that happened in service, but it also shortens the time to degree, saving the student time and money. It's a very tangible way to honor their background.

In summary, Col. (Ret.) Mike Carrell's perspective is that of a systems builder. He took an enormous university and said, "We're going to make this a welcoming home for veterans." And he succeeded. His work gives me hope because it shows that the problems are not insurmountable. They are, in fact, solvable with leadership, planning, and heart.

Every time I walk into a university veterans center nowadays, bustling with activity, I think of people like Mike Carrell and Don Accamando, who laid the groundwork. Yet, as Carrell himself would be first to say, there's more to be done, and many schools are still catching up. The torch is now being carried by the next generation of innovators, which brings me to another fascinating conversation I had. One with a retired general who is leveraging technology to revolutionize how veterans learn and train for new careers.

Immersive Technology for Transition

Brig. Gen. (Ret.) Stewart Rodeheaver focuses on technology-based training solutions. After a distinguished thirty-eight-year Army career, including commanding troops in Iraq, Rodeheaver could have ridden off into retirement. Instead, he founded a technology company and dove headfirst into the world of VR, augmented reality (AR), and AI-driven learning.

His mission? To make training more effective for the newest generation of military members and to bridge the gap as they become veterans reentering the civilian workforce. I had the privilege of interviewing Rodeheaver, and I came away convinced that immersive learning tools are going to play a big role in improving veteran education and employment transitions.

One of the first points Rodeheaver made was that traditional classroom methods often fail veterans and service members because that's just not how they're conditioned to learn. "In the military, they're not trained with someone in a book and a person standing up just talking to them with slides, a technique many of our veterans refer to as 'death by PowerPoint.' If you do that, you lose them very quickly," he told me bluntly.

Military training is hands-on, fast-paced, and immersive. You learn by doing, under stress, with all your senses engaged. So, when a veteran walks into a college lecture hall where a professor drones on for ninety minutes, or a job training seminar that's all PowerPoint, it can be painfully disengaging.

Rodeheaver's insight is that multisensory, active learning isn't just a preference, and it may be key to unlocking veterans' potential in post-service education. "That's what the key to this is. Get them out there. And extended reality is absolutely the best way to do that," he said, referring to the umbrella of VR/AR tech.

He's actually seen veterans with TBI make greater gains in relearning skills when using VR, because the technology engages sight, sound, touch with haptic feedback, and even motion, stimulating neural pathways and muscle memory in ways traditional study can't. As a rehabilitation physician, I found that incredibly exciting. It's a bit like tricking the brain into learning faster by making it think it's in the scenario.

Rodeheaver's company, Vizitech USA, has applied this approach to various fields. He described one project where they created a virtual first-responder training program for emergency medical technicians (EMTs) and firefighters. Instead of using mannequins or staged drills that get interrupted whenever a real call comes in, trainees can don VR gear and find themselves at a lifelike accident scene.

There are virtual victims who talk, thanks to AI. If you ask a question such as "Where does it hurt?" the victim will answer in real time. The trainee can practice the entire sequence of care, and the system reacts to their actions. If they put a tourniquet on the wrong wound and ignore a chest wound, the patient's condition worsens to simulate what would happen.

It's a safe space to learn from mistakes and is far more effective than multiple-choice tests or listening to a lecture about triage. Rodeheaver explained that the AI-driven virtual patients even respond to incorrect treatments, guiding trainees to realize and correct their errors. As he put it, if you tell them something wrong, they'll correct you. The result is that by the time these trainees face a real emergency, they've essentially been there already in VR.

Now, translate this to veterans' transitions. Think of a combat medic leaving the service. Someone like Matt Garrett, whom I referenced in the last chapter, for example. Instead of plopping him into an entry-level biology class and hoping he toughs it out, what if we could offer him an immersive bridge program? Rodeheaver and I discussed the idea of using VR to help veterans capitalize on their military skills and see a pathway to civilian jobs.

For instance, his team built a virtual auto garage with different car engines. You can take apart a virtual engine with haptic tools, and it feels real, but you don't need a physical engine or shop space. A veteran who was a vehicle mechanic in the Army could use that to get certified more quickly in automotive repair.

Or a former Navy corpsman could practice in a virtual ER, interacting with virtual patients, as preparation for EMT certification or nursing school. The possibilities are endless. Rodeheaver mentioned they even created virtual electric car and aircraft engine training for schools that couldn't afford the real equipment setups. This not only saves money, but it also removes physical barriers. A veteran in a remote area could put on a headset and learn to weld or repair factory machines without needing the actual machinery on site.

From Rodeheaver's perspective, technology can also ease the cultural transition for veterans. His work is a reminder that innovation should be a part of the veteran support conversation. It's not just about more counseling or extended deadlines; it's also about fundamentally reimagining how we deliver education and training. With VR and AI, we now have tools that can personalize and accelerate learning for veterans in ways that were science fiction a generation ago.

Rodeheaver's core message is that our Guardians are doers and experiential learners and that if we teach and train them with that understanding, their transition can be much smoother. By embracing immersive technologies, we can reduce the "square peg in a round hole" problem. Instead, we can create square holes for our square-peg veterans, where they fit and flourish.

Guiding Transitions with Heart and Strategy

This brings me to my conversation with U.S. Air Force Lt. Col. (Ret.) Don Accamando, Ed.D., a scholar and practitioner in the realm of veteran transitions. He founded the Office for Military and Veteran Students at Duquesne University and even wrote his doctoral thesis on the specific transition needs of military students. When I spoke with Accamando, I could sense the heart he has for our Guardians, as well as the no-nonsense strategy he believes is needed to fix the system.

One of Accamando's chief arguments is that, as I've mentioned earlier, we must devote far more time and effort to the "handoff" from military to civilian life, particularly in the realm of education and employment. He noted that currently, a service member might spend months in basic training, but only a few days in the TAP learning how to be a civilian. That imbalance is glaring.

Echoing the words of Army veteran Adam Peters (mentioned earlier), Accamando insists we need something akin to a second boot camp to reorient the individual for the next chapter of life. In practical terms, he suggests comprehensive transition counseling that includes aptitude testing, one-on-one interviews, and a personalized road map for each service member.

Accamando's vision is to essentially catch every service member before they exit, sit them down, and ask: "What do you really want to do? What are you good at? What do you need to get there? Let's find the right school or training or opportunity for you, in a location that makes sense, and let's connect you with the people who can help."

It's intensive, yes, but it could save so much pain later. As Accamando colorfully put it to me, it truly takes a village to get these men and women aimed in the right direction because there is just too much red tape and noise for them to navigate alone. I couldn't agree more. We can't expect a twenty-two-year-old who's been living a very structured military life to suddenly become a career and education planning expert on their own.

At Duquesne University, Accamando practiced what he preached. He established an office that not only processes GI Bill paperwork but also addresses the social, financial, and academic needs of its military-affiliated students, operating under a holistic mission. When I visited, I saw how they had liaisons in the registrar and bursar's offices specifically to handle veterans' enrollment and billing issues, so that no veteran gets tangled in bureaucracy alone.

Accamando admitted that even he, as the director, doesn't try to personally keep up with every twist and turn of GI Bill policy. Instead, he has those specialist liaisons and contacts at the VA he can call on when a student vet hits a snag. This was a smart revelation, and it makes me think that perhaps every school needs a dedicated "VA benefits navigator" who stays updated on rules and can sort out issues quickly. Without that, schools could misfile certifying paperwork, or veterans would miss out on benefits simply because nobody on campus is alerted to the changes in the process. Accamando's approach at Duquesne ensured veterans aren't left alone to decipher their benefits; the school takes on that burden as a partner.

Accamando is also a big proponent of creating a sense of community for veterans in academia. He often talks about building a "fire team" or squad mentality in school, encouraging veterans to band together and support one another academically and socially. Under his guidance, Duquesne's Student Veterans Association became very active, and events such as its annual 5K run for veterans draw in not just vets but also civilian students and faculty.

Policy-wise, Accamando had a few pointed recommendations. He strongly feels that some policies need to be more flexible to account for young service members' lack of foresight. For example, regarding boot camp GI Bill sign-up, Don argued to me that there absolutely should be an appeals or second-chance process for those who initially decline but later realize they need the benefit.

"An eighteen- or nineteen-year-old cannot decide his/her future on the spot in boot camp," he said emphatically. I heartily agree. Let them enroll later, even if it requires some extra contribution; it's better than shutting them out for life. Don also mentioned the transferability issue, as a lot of service members didn't know they had to transfer their GI Bill to a spouse or child while still in service, so they never did and lost that chance.

This again comes down to poor communication of complex rules. He suggests a grace period for recent vets to make a transfer election after discharge, given how often people miss that window. These are the kinds of veteran-friendly tweaks that could be implemented if the voices of people like Accamando reach the ears of policymakers.

Practical Steps Forward

What I appreciate most about Accamando's perspective is that it's both compassionate and practical. He doesn't just say, "We should help vets because it's the right thing to do." He also says, "Here's exactly how we can do it better, step by step." And he's implemented those steps at the university level, proving they work. Duquesne isn't the largest school in the country, but what Accamando has done there could be scaled up anywhere.

In fact, many of his ideas mirror what Mike Carrell did at OSU, just tuned to a smaller campus. This tells me there's a converging consensus among those who have figured this out. The consensus is dedicated resources, knowledgeable staff, veteran-to-veteran mentorship, tailored counseling, and policy flexibility. These are the ingredients for a successful transition program.

As I synthesize all these insights from Matt Garrett's on-the-ground truth, Mike Carrell's institutional reforms, Stewart Rodeheaver's technological innovations, and Don Accamando's holistic counseling, I see how they all interconnect. It becomes a vision of an ideal journey for a veteran:

- Before leaving service, they get thorough counseling to chart an education/employment path that suits them, with any needed benefits explained clearly and all paperwork squared away.
- Upon entering school, they find a campus ready to receive them, and a strong veterans center that helps with integration, credits, and community building.
- In the classroom or training workshop, they engage with modern, interactive learning that keeps them motivated and translates their military skills into new knowledge.
- Throughout the process, they have peers and mentors, so they never feel alone in that hole.

This, to me, is the road map for guarding our Guardians in education and beyond. And it's not a pipe dream. It's already happening in pockets around the country. Our job is to expand those pockets until they become the standard everywhere.

CHAPTER 9

EDUCATION AS THE NEW MISSION

The military's transition programs have traditionally focused on basic briefings about benefits and job hunting, but they often leave our Guardians on their own to navigate the maze of college admissions and GI Bill paperwork. We must change that.

We should bring educators onto the military bases as part of the transition process. Imagine college counselors and VA education specialists stationed at major bases like Fort Bragg or Camp Pendleton, available to meet one-on-one with those about to leave service. During the final six to twelve months of service, troops interested in school could be guided through choosing a field of study, finding the right institution, and filling out forms for admission and benefits.

This would be a bit like a high school college counseling office, as for many enlistees, the military was their "college" experience right out of high school. Now, as they prepare to reenter the civilian world, they need the same kind of personalized guidance an eighteen-year-old college-bound senior would get.

Service branches should partner with local colleges and state university systems to provide on-base academic advising. Before discharge, every service member should have the chance to explore education options with a counselor who understands both the GI Bill and the academic world.

We should conduct aptitude tests and skills translators to help identify careers or majors that fit each veteran's interests and military experience. Also, we must evaluate the individual's military training for potential college credit. Many states and schools now grant academic credit for certain military courses or technical skills,[99] and our Guardians should know about these to avoid repeating coursework.

The GI Bill application and enrollment certification process should be simplified and started before separation when possible. The VA and the DOW can collaborate so that a service member's GI Bill benefits are pre-certified to start immediately upon school enrollment. No waiting months for the first housing allowance to arrive.

Above all, this transition period needs to be hands-on. We often talk about veterans reintegrating into civilian life, but from the veteran's perspective, it's more like starting from scratch. They left home as teenagers, spent formative years in the tightly structured world of the military, and now find themselves back in an unstructured civilian society that has moved on without them. It is unrealistic to expect them to navigate higher education's bureaucracy solo.

Creating Veteran-Friendly Campuses

Because stepping onto a college campus can be an overwhelming culture shock for veterans academically, socially, and emotionally, universities must recognize this and adapt their environments to be truly veteran-friendly. What does that mean in practice? It's more than just waiving application fees or giving lip service on Veterans Day. It

99 "Get Academic Credit for Military Training," Illinois Department of Veterans Affairs, accessed August 5, 2025, https://veterans.illinois.gov/services-benefits/education/get-academic-credit-for-military-training.html.

means creating programs, spaces, and policies that meet veterans where they are.

A key feature of veteran-friendly campuses is a physical veterans center—a space on campus where vets can gather, study quietly, and find staff who can answer questions. These centers often serve as one-stop shops for GI Bill certification, advising, tutoring referrals, and simply camaraderie.

For example, OSU (the nation's largest campus, located in a state with one of the highest veteran populations) opened a comprehensive veterans support office when it saw a surge of GI Bill students. It became a model for how a big university can make a large campus feel smaller and more navigable for those who served. On the opposite coast, the University of Southern California and the University of California, Los Angeles (UCLA), were early leaders in establishing veteran resource centers, recognizing the large military community in Southern California. These efforts show that whether a school has fifty veteran students or five hundred, having a dedicated space and staff for them is immensely helpful.

Many campuses now have chapters of Student Veterans of America (SVA) or similar clubs where veteran students can connect socially. But mentorship can go further, pairing incoming vets with those who are further along in their studies can create a battle-buddy system on campus. Upperclassmen veterans can help newcomers with everything from navigating course registration to finding off-campus housing. Universities should facilitate these connections, as they provide both practical help and a sense of belonging.

Remember that about one in four veterans has experienced TBI during their service.[100] This can mean memory issues, difficulty con-

100 Justin E. Karr et al., "Traumatic Brain Injury in U.S. Veterans: Prevalence and Associations with Physical, Mental, and Cognitive Health," *Archives of Physical Medicine and Rehabilitation* 106, no. 4 (April 2025): 537–47, https://doi.org/10.1016/j.apmr.2024.11.010.

centrating, or other learning challenges, even if the veteran appears fine outwardly. Campus disability services and tutoring centers must be prepared to accommodate these needs. That could mean offering note-taking services, extra time on tests, or simply training tutors to understand PTSD/TBI symptoms.

Educating the educators about these invisible disabilities is crucial. Professors should know that if a veteran asks for help or seems disengaged, there might be more at play, and flexibility can make the difference between that student thriving or dropping out of school.

Perhaps the biggest cultural challenge on campus for our Guardians is isolation. Universities can ease this by fostering understanding on both sides. Encourage faculty to incorporate veterans' perspectives in class discussions without singling them out uncomfortably, and educate traditional students about the value that veteran classmates bring.

Some campuses offer "green zone" training for faculty/staff, similar to safe zone training for other populations, to raise awareness of military culture and support for veterans. The more the campus community appreciates veterans as assets, the more vets will feel welcome to share their insights rather than stay silent and withdrawn.

Crucially, schools should also be mindful of campus climate. For instance, extremely politicized or chaotic campus environments can be jarring for vets. It's not that veterans can't handle debate, but imagine being a newly discharged soldier who narrowly survived combat, only to hear classmates casually proclaim anti-military sentiments or engage in disruptive protests.

Some veterans have reported feeling unwelcome or even hostile vibes on campuses where the military is viewed with suspicion. We must bridge that divide with dialogue and education. Meanwhile, veterans themselves should have a support network like the Vet

Lounge or club to retreat to when campus life feels alien. No one wants to feel like an outsider in their own school.

Ultimately, community colleges and smaller schools play a crucial role in this context. Not every veteran will jump straight into a big four-year university, and that's OK. In fact, starting at a community college can be a smart choice, especially for those who need to re-hone their study skills or prefer a smaller setting. Community colleges are generally more accustomed to adult learners and often provide more flexible scheduling. We should celebrate and strengthen veteran programs at these two-year institutions.

Matching Military Skills to Academic Pathways

One of the saddest wastes of talent is when a Guardian is not guided to leverage the skills and passions they developed in uniform. Military service often imparts specialized training and a sense of purpose. Yet too often, that experience isn't translated into a satisfying educational path.

Earlier, I shared the story of Navy Corpsman Matt Garrett, who absolutely loved his role providing medical care in the field. By the time he left the service, he had effectively been an EMT, a nurse, even a battlefield medic under extreme pressure. In a just world, Garrett's transition would have been seamless.

He could have gone straight into a nursing program or pre-med track, received credit for some of his military medical training, and been on a fast track to becoming a licensed nurse or physician. In fact, he was likely only a couple of years away from a six-figure career in the civilian medical field—something both he and society would benefit from immensely.

Instead, what happened? Garrett ended up drifting into a completely unrelated field because that was what was available and easy to enroll in at the time. He wasn't presented with options to continue in the medical field. No one sat him down to say, "You know, with your experience, you could become a registered nurse in two years, or a physician in six. Here are the steps."

To turn this around, colleges and vocational programs must proactively match veterans' military skills to academic pathways. Some actionable measures include the following:

- **Military-to-civilian skill translators:** Develop tools or improve existing ones that can take a veteran's military occupational specialty or role and suggest corresponding majors or certifications. For instance, an Army medic or Navy corpsman should be informed about nursing programs, EMT courses, or pre-med possibilities. A logistics specialist from the Marines might be pointed toward supply chain management or business administration degrees. These suggestions should be included in transition counseling and reinforced by college advisors.

- **Academic credit for service training:** As mentioned earlier, many veterans can get college credit for courses they took in the service. Each branch issues transcripts that universities can evaluate. States such as Illinois have laws or policies requiring public colleges to award credit for certain military experiences.[101] Schools should not wait for veterans to ask. They should automatically review military transcripts upon admission and inform the student, "You've just been awarded nine credits for your military leadership course and medic training," for example. This not only shortens the time to graduation but also validates the veteran's prior learning.

101 Illinois Department of Veterans Affairs, "Get Academic Credit for Military Training."

- **Career counseling that listens:** Rather than shunting veterans into generic business or liberal arts degrees because they're "easy," advisors should take the time to ask each veteran, "What do you really want to do? What did you enjoy or dislike about your time in service?" If a veteran doesn't want anything to do with their military job, that's fine. But if they did love aspects of their service, we should show them how those can morph into a civilian career.

The benefit of matching skills to academics affirms to the veteran that their service prepared them for something, rather than made them feel like they're behind their civilian peers. Instead of starting from zero, they realize they're starting ahead in many ways, with discipline, real-world experience, and applicable knowledge. This boosts confidence and gives a sense of purpose to their studies. Education then becomes not a random detour but the next chapter of their mission.

Leveraging Nonprofits and Alliances

While I've addressed what schools and government should do, equally important is the role of nonprofit organizations, foundations, and even alumni groups in driving change. In the realm of veteran education, nonprofits have the freedom to innovate and fill gaps that bureaucratic institutions sometimes can't move quickly enough to fill. We've already seen some stellar examples of this.

One standout is the National Veterans Leadership Foundation (NVLF). This organization, led by forward-thinking veterans and educators like Col. (Ret.) Mike Carrell and others, has forged partnerships across universities to share best practices and develop new programs. The NVLF helped launch a nationwide network of military/veteran office directors from diverse campuses, effectively creating a brain trust of experts dedicated to supporting military-connected students.[102]

By connecting these professionals, a good idea at one school can rapidly spread to others. The NVLF's approach also includes partnering with and supporting regional alliances. For example, in Ohio, it united over fifty public and private colleges in a statewide consortium focused on enhancing support for military students. The Big Ten Conference schools have banded together through the NVLF to offer unparalleled access to programs and opportunities for student veterans across state lines.[103]

This is groundbreaking. It means a veteran at, say, Indiana University can tap into resources or programs at UCLA or Penn State thanks to cross-campus collaboration. Such alliances break down silos and ensure that no veteran falls through the cracks simply because they chose one school over another.

Another innovative nonprofit effort uses the cultural power of sports to raise awareness and support for veterans in education. Recognizing that athletes and warriors share common struggles, some veteran groups have partnered with college athletic departments. They use the popularity of football events to highlight veterans' issues and even recruit former service members into new roles, such as coaching internships or team mentorship roles. This not only provides vets with a sense of camaraderie and purpose on campus but also educates student-athletes about service and sacrifice. It's a creative example of thinking outside the box to integrate veterans into campus life in a positive, visible way.

Alumni networks are another untapped resource. Universities listen closely to their alumni because, after all, alumni donations and

102 "Campus Leadership," National Veterans Leadership Foundation, accessed August 5, 2025, https://nvlf.us/campus-leadership/.

103 "Campus Leadership."

advocacy often drive institutional priorities. If you're a civilian reading this book and you're an alumnus of a college, you can help. Find out if your alma mater has a veterans program or a veterans services office. If it does, reach out and ask how you can support it. Maybe you could mentor a student veteran or sponsor a scholarship.

If it doesn't have a visible program, consider nudging the alumni association or administration to start one. Even simply raising the question, "What are we doing to help our student veterans succeed?" can plant a seed on a campus that hasn't focused on the issue. Remember, many college leaders and faculty might have little direct exposure to the military. They may not realize a problem exists unless someone points it out. Alumni have clout, so use yours to make veteran education a priority.

Nonprofits can also assist with very practical needs, such as bridge funding and emergency assistance. Organizations such as SVA chapters or local charities can create emergency funds or zero-interest loan programs to help veterans bridge short-term financial gaps. Those stopgaps can prevent a temporary cash crunch from snowballing into a full-blown crisis of homelessness or dropout. Additionally, nonprofits often provide free services, such as textbook lending libraries for veterans or grants for buying a laptop or other school supplies. These may seem small, but they remove barriers and signal to veterans that people have their backs.

Sustaining the Change

While grassroots efforts and campus-level programs are critical, we also need top-down leadership and policy changes to institutionalize progress. One issue is the inconsistency that can arise when a supportive leader leaves and a new one takes their place. In the military, command changes every couple of years, and sadly, good initiatives sometimes die on the vine because a new commander wants to do things "their own way."

We must encourage, if not demand, that the DOW and individual base commanders prioritize transition programs as a matter of policy, not personal preference. Ideally, successful pilot programs, such as inviting employers and college representatives on base, should be standardized across all bases. The Pentagon should issue guidance that education counseling is a required component of out-processing.

Similarly, in higher education, college presidents and deans should visibly champion their veteran students. When the tone is set from the top, it empowers mid-level staff to push for needed resources. We've seen schools that, once they earned a Military Friendly School designation or were recognized in Best for Vets rankings, doubled down on those efforts because it became a point of pride. Leadership should also measure outcomes: *Are our student veterans graduating? Are they getting the help they need?* Making those metrics part of a school's success indicators will keep attention on the issue even if key personnel change.

On the federal side, the VA can continue to improve the GI Bill administration. Recent IT upgrades and better inter-agency data sharing have made a difference, but there's still room to grow. The VA should aim for zero delays in benefit payments—a goal that may require more staffing or better systems, but one worth pursuing so that no one has to beg or borrow money to eat while waiting for a check.

Moreover, Congress and the VA might consider extending certain GI Bill timelines or giving more flexibility. For instance, if a veteran has a health relapse or personal issue that interrupts school, they should be able to pause and restart benefits without penalty. The focus should be on completion and success, not arbitrary time limits.

Another policy angle is to incentivize colleges to recruit and support veterans. The federal government could provide grants or bonus funding to institutions that have high veteran graduation rates or innovative veteran programs. Essentially, make it attractive for colleges to become excellent in this arena. After World War II, many colleges rolled out the red carpet for veterans because they represented a huge influx of enrollment and tuition dollars.

Today's numbers are smaller, but not insignificant. Over six hundred thousand veterans or family members use GI Bill benefits each year.[104] That's a substantial student population spread across the country. We should encourage schools to view veteran students as assets and actively compete to serve them well.

Finally, leadership must come from the veterans themselves. This doesn't mean they should have to fix the system. They already did their part by serving. But veteran voices are powerful in advocating for change. Many of the improvements we've highlighted started because veterans spoke up. They told their stories to college administrators, formed a committee, wrote op-eds, or testified to Congress about what isn't working.

When our Guardians band together to demand better transitions, people listen. If you are a veteran who struggled in your education journey, consider sharing your experience with those in charge. Your honesty could spur a program that makes it easier for the next person.

A Call to Arms and Minds

Education can be the turning point that launches a veteran into a fulfilling civilian life. It was for the World War II generation, and it can be for the post-9/11 generation, but only if we rally to make it so.

104 Prestianni, "71 Military and Veteran Higher Education Statistics for 2025."

- **To colleges and universities:** Educate yourselves about your veteran students, then educate your campus to embrace and support them. Build the structures, from orientation classes to vet centers, that will help them thrive. You have everything to gain by investing in these driven, mature, resilient learners.
- **To the DOW and the VA:** Make the handoff from service member to student as smooth as possible. Start the education process on the base, streamline the benefits, and don't let red tape thwart the very outcomes that the GI Bill was designed to achieve.
- **To communities and nonprofits:** Keep innovating. If a veteran falls through the cracks, be there with a net—whether it's a scholarship, a mentoring program, or just a place to belong. Your agility and passion can solve problems that big institutions haven't yet solved.
- **To alumni and citizens:** Use your voice. Ask your local colleges about their veteran support. Thank a veteran student for their service and encourage them in their studies. Sometimes a simple acknowledgment can make them feel seen and valued on a campus where they might otherwise feel invisible.
- **To veterans embarking on education:** Know that you are not alone. Others have walked this path and succeeded, and you can too. Don't hesitate to seek out your campus veteran office, join the SVA chapter, or speak up if you're struggling. Your next mission is to invest in yourself, and you've earned every bit of help along the way. Remember that the qualities

that got you through military training and deployments are the same ones that will carry you through a calculus class or a term paper.

Fifteen years from now, I envision a world where veteran education support is so ingrained that it's almost unremarkable. Imagine a young soldier at Fort Hood sitting down with a counselor six months before discharge and mapping out a plan to attend Texas A&M. By the time she leaves the Army, she's already registered for classes, connected with a student-veteran mentor on campus, and secured housing with her GI Bill allowance ready to kick in.

On campus, professors know her by name because the veterans' office gave them a heads-up that she's coming from combat service and might need a little acclimation period. She finds refuge in the veterans center between classes, where she meets other former service members from different eras and branches, sharing jokes and study tips. When she encounters bureaucratic hiccups, they get resolved quickly by knowledgeable staff, so she can stay focused on learning.

Over the next four years, she not only earns her degree but also finds a new sense of community and purpose. On graduation day, she walks across that stage with pride, cheered on by family, professors, and her fellow vets. She's ready for the next chapter, whether that's a career or further education, and perhaps most importantly, she knows she's not fighting alone anymore.

This is the future we can achieve if we turn these ideas into action. Education for our Guardians is not a favor we grant; it's a continuation of their service, an opportunity for our nation to reap the rewards of their talents in new ways. Every veteran who graduates and goes on to a successful civilian career is a win, not just for them, but for all of us. It strengthens families, communities, and our country as a whole.

The sustainability of our all-volunteer force depends on this too. Young people considering military service watch how we treat today's veterans. If they see veterans struggling and unsupported in post-military life, they will think twice about enlisting. Conversely, if they see that serving your country is followed by a smooth path to a college degree and a good job, they'll be more inclined to raise their hand.

> Education for our Guardians is not a favor we grant; it's a continuation of their service, an opportunity for our nation to reap the rewards of their talents in new ways.

We must remember that our veterans have already proven they can do amazing things under the toughest conditions. They've led troops, saved lives, mastered complex technologies, and navigated foreign cultures. Gaining a college education is simply the next arena for them to apply those gifts.

Our job as a society is to remove the unnecessary obstacles and cheer them on. This mission calls for new ideas, bold actions, and unwavering commitment from all of us. Together, we can ensure that every veteran who dreams of a diploma earns one, and that in doing so, they find a new sense of mission, identity, and success in the country they defended.

SECTION IV

EMPLOYMENT

CHAPTER 10

FROM COMBAT TO CUBICLE

One of the first barriers to employment that our Guardians encounter is misperception. Many civilian employers have stereotypes. Some see veterans as rigid order-takers, while others view them as broken or volatile. There is a persistent gap in understanding military experience. As one analysis noted, over 60 percent of our Guardians are underemployed, working below their potential, which reflects "a systemic undervaluation of military experience in the corporate world."[105]

In practice, this means employers often fail to see how leadership in a combat unit or logistical expertise in the field translates to leadership in an office or project management in a company. Veterans sense this dismissal. All of that work, all of that intellectual property that you had, doesn't seem to matter.

The same applies to the job hunt. Hiring managers might not recognize the value of leading a platoon under pressure or maintaining million-dollar equipment. Instead, they might assume a veteran's

105 Jonathan Due, "America Solved Veterans' Unemployment Within a Decade—but 'Underemployment' Continues to Hold Back Their Talents," Raymond A. Mason School of Business, November 11, 2024, https://mason.wm.edu/news/2024/america-solved-veterans-unemployment-within-a-decade-but-underemployment-continues-to-hold-back-their-talents.php.

skills are too niche or too "military" and not applicable to business. Nothing could be further from the truth. Veterans are problem-solvers, team players, and dedicated workers. Yet the civilian hiring process often overlooks this.

According to "The State of the American Veteran" study, "Nearly 70 percent of pre-9/11 and 74 percent of post-9/11 veterans did not have a job when they left the military."[106] This study notes that:

> Post-9/11 veterans are nearly twice as likely as pre-9/11 veterans to be employed full-time, yet only half of post-9/11 veterans surveyed reported working full-time. While 50% of post-9/11 veterans are employed full-time, only 30% of pre-9/11 veterans are employed full-time. Post-9/11 veterans are also over twice as likely to be working part-time (10%) as pre-9/11 veterans (5%). It should be noted that pre-9/11 veterans are over ten times more likely to report being retired (34%) than are pre-9/11 veterans (3%).[107]

Those numbers are staggering, and a 2024 Veterans Day report further highlighted that while veteran unemployment is low, almost half of veterans describe their transition to civilian life as "difficult" or "very difficult."[108] This difficulty persists not because veterans lack ability, but because employers lack understanding of military training, military values, and military culture. Too few companies truly invest in learning how a military resume can enrich their workforce.

106 Carl Andrew Castro et al., *The State of the American Veteran: The Orange County Veterans Study* (University of Southern California, Center for Innovation and Research on Veterans & Military Families, 2015), https://cir.usc.edu/wp-content/uploads/2015/02/OC-Veterans-Study_USC-CIR_Feb-2015.pdf.

107 Castro et al., *The State of the American Veteran.*

108 Due, "America Solved Veterans' Unemployment Within a Decade."

Compounding this is a practice I've personally witnessed: companies that treat veteran hiring as a check-the-box exercise rather than a commitment. Some large firms proudly announce veteran hiring initiatives, yet quietly cycle those hires out after grabbing a tax credit. I once pointed out that one well-known company was praised annually by Congress for hiring veterans, but fewer than 15 percent of those veterans were employed for a year.

In essence, many of those Guardians were hired for a PR boost or incentive and then left adrift. They were hired but not truly *employed*. We will explore this difference more in chapter 11, but it's important to note here that some of the veterans we encounter sense when they are a token hire rather than a valued team member, reinforcing their feeling of being misunderstood.

> Some veterans sense when they are a token hire rather than a valued team member, reinforcing their feeling of being misunderstood.

The reward–benefit ratio of genuinely employing veterans is incredible. Companies benefit immensely from veterans' work ethic and skills. But first, those Guardians must be given a real chance, not just a short-term slot.

The Skills Translation Gap

A related challenge is the translation of military skills to civilian jobs. Military roles often have no direct civilian equivalent in title. A medic may not realize how to market their experience as healthcare leadership or emergency management. An infantry squad leader has been responsible for lives and complex operations, but to a civilian HR rep scanning a resume, that might just look like "team leader with no corporate experience."

Veterans often need help articulating their skills in terms that civilian employers understand. In fact, 50 percent of veterans and active military members find it difficult to translate their military experience into a resume.[109] Half of our Guardians struggle just to explain what they know in a way that the civilian hiring systems recognize. That's a startling statistic. And it isn't for lack of ability; it's due to a lack of guidance and understanding. Too often, the burden is entirely on the veteran to "civilianize" their resume, rather than on employers to recognize the value of military experience.

I have seen this firsthand in higher education and employment alike. A while back, I had a wonderful conversation with Carson Rowland. He enlisted right out of high school at seventeen, entering boot camp in September 2018 and graduating that November.

Assigned as a fireman, his responsibility was maintaining weapon systems on the electronic side. He attended electronics school in the Great Lakes region, where he excelled and earned a Navy enlisted certification, a specialized qualification. His designation was as a Mark 160 Tech, working on the gun computer system for the five-inch gun mounted on destroyers and cruisers. After completing his training in Virginia Beach—where he graduated as an honor student and top of his class—he reported to his ship in September 2019, just one year after joining.

Thanks to Reserve Officers' Training Corps experience in high school and the Navy's advanced pipeline rules, Rowland quickly advanced in rank. He entered boot camp as an E3, was promoted to E4 after completing A school in June 2019, and by the time he reached his ship, he was already eligible to sit for the E5 exam. Scoring in the

109 "Veterans Fear PTSD Stigmas," Provider Information Management System, February 8, 2023, https://pimsyehr.com/veterans-fear-ptsd-stigmas/.

99th percentile, he was promoted to E5 in early 2020, just over a year after enlisting, an unusually fast rise for someone so young.

Despite his academic struggles in high school, which were partly due to being a year younger than his peers, Rowland demonstrated strong technical aptitude in the Navy upon graduation with a 2.3 GPA. His success in advanced training programs was not reflected in his college applications, however, and many universities and colleges judged him primarily on his GPA.

Unable to fully capture his Navy achievements in an essay, he instead enrolled at Columbus State Community College, where the Student Veterans Association president personally invited him to get involved. In a small, supportive environment, Rowland's military background was seen as an asset, not an obstacle. This lesson applies to employers: Recognition and mentorship can make a world of difference. One bright spot is that some companies and programs have begun to step up.

Public–Private Partnerships

Public–private partnerships after the Great Recession led to initiatives that hired hundreds of thousands of veterans and established veteran transition institutes at universities.[110] Those efforts slashed the post-9/11 veteran unemployment rate from over 12 percent down to under 3 percent in recent years.[111] We have addressed the unemployment crisis with these measures, but now we face the next front: underemployment and mismatch. Veterans have the talent; we need to place them where they can use it.

Translating skills isn't just a paperwork issue; it's psychological too. Our Guardians often underrate themselves. Dave Hartman, a

110 Due, "America Solved Veterans' Unemployment Within a Decade."

111 Due, "America Solved Veterans' Unemployment Within a Decade."

quiet Army veteran I interviewed, admitted that when he first came home, he had no understanding of what he had just been through.

Hartman is a U.S. Army veteran who served as a tank crewman during the Gulf War, entering the military just two weeks after high school at age seventeen. He went on to complete two years of active duty and nine years with the Ohio National Guard, experiences that taught him resilience, accountability, and the power of teamwork.

That said, it took him over a decade to process his own experience and see its value. Think about that: If veterans themselves aren't immediately recognizing how extraordinary their own backgrounds are, how can we expect civilian employers to? We need better support right at that transition moment to help veterans frame their experiences in empowering ways.

> If veterans themselves aren't immediately recognizing how extraordinary their own backgrounds are, how can we expect civilian employers to?

Too often, we send them off with a brief TAP and a handshake. It's not enough, and this gap leaves our Guardians alone in translating and marketing their skills. No wonder so many end up in jobs far below their capability or bounce between short-term positions.

But these challenges are not insurmountable. Some solutions, such as skill translators and career counselors specializing in veteran resumes, are emerging. We will discuss concrete recommendations in chapter 12. For now, the key point is that the civilian workforce doesn't automatically recognize military talent, and we must bridge that gap deliberately.

The tragedy is not that veterans have nothing to offer. I would argue they often have more leadership and technical training that has been tried and proven than in the private sector. In addition, they have been trained in core values and in the invaluable LDRSHIP traits—Loyalty, Duty, Respect, Selfless Service, Honor, Integrity, and Personal Courage.

As one survey found, 92 percent of military job seekers believe their service makes them better employees, yet only 60 percent feel their military background helps in their civilian job search.[112] That disparity and confidence in their abilities versus actual job-search benefit highlights the translation problem. Veterans know they're capable; we need employers to understand it too.

Nonprofit Partnerships

From a nonprofit perspective, The Three Rangers Foundation stands as a bridge for those who have served in the 75th Ranger Regiment, ensuring that the transition from military service to civilian life is not faced alone. Executive Director and Cmd. Sgt. Maj. (Ret.) Mike Hall translated his extensive military service of thirty-four years into a nonprofit assisting fellow Rangers with transitioning into civilian life.

Their mission is clear: to provide mentorship, resources, and meaningful connections that equip Rangers and their families for long-term success. By surrounding Rangers with a supportive community, the foundation helps them navigate the practical and personal challenges that come with leaving active service. Whether it's education, employment, or personal development, the organization is committed to ensuring every Ranger thrives beyond their time in uniform.

The Four Pillars of the Three Rangers Foundation embody the spirit and values that guide everything the organization does.

112 Provider Information Management System, "Veterans Fear PTSD Stigmas."

- The Gold Star holds the highest place of honor, reminding us of the ultimate sacrifice made by Rangers who gave their lives in service, and the families who carry their legacy with courage and resilience.

- The Compass serves as a steadying force, ensuring that all actions remain rooted in what is legal, ethical, and moral, while reinforcing the personal responsibility each Ranger carries for their choices.

- The Lightning Bolt reflects the boldness and urgency ingrained in the Ranger creed, a commitment to take decisive action when opportunities arise, harnessing power and precision to create impact.

- Finally, the Parachute symbolizes a life fully lived, defined by adventure, risk, and the willingness to leap into the unknown in pursuit of something greater.[113]

At the heart of this work is the mentorship program, which pairs Rangers with experienced professionals who understand the unique challenges of military transition. These relationships go beyond simple career advice, offering guidance, encouragement, and a sense of belonging during a critical life stage.

By offering mentorship, access to resources, and a community of peers who share the same values, the organization provides a consistent base during what can otherwise be a daunting season of change. What sets the foundation apart is its deep understanding of the Ranger experience and the bonds forged in service. Mentors within the program know firsthand the discipline, grit, and loyalty it takes to

113 "Who We Are," Three Rangers Foundation, accessed September 8, 2025, https://www.threerangersfoundation.org/who-we-are.

be a Ranger, and they help translate those qualities into opportunities in civilian life.

Whether it's connecting someone to a professional network, guiding them through educational opportunities, or simply being a sounding board during tough times, the foundation ensures that every Ranger is equipped not just to survive but to thrive long after leaving active duty.

Fear, Stigma, and Invisible Injuries

Beyond skill mismatch, fear and stigma often shadow veterans in the job market. Hollywood-fueled myths of the "unstable veteran" and sensational media coverage of PTSD have created trepidation among some employers. Veterans sense this. According to a LiveCareer survey, 87.7 percent of veterans believe PTSD or other mental injuries of war affect their employment chances when returning to civilian work.[114]

In other words, nearly nine in ten veterans think they're being judged for invisible wounds before they even get in the door. Are they right? Unfortunately, sometimes yes. "When it comes to PTSD and other injuries of war, military job seekers think employers are still in the dark," said one veteran employment advocate, noting that 93 percent of veterans say employers need better education on these issues.[115] I agree wholeheartedly.

The average employer might think PTSD is a ticking time bomb, when in reality, the vast majority of veterans (over 80 percent) do not have PTSD.[116] Yet, employers may not realize that 6 percent of

114 Provider Information Management System, "Veterans Fear PTSD Stigmas."

115 Provider Information Management System, "Veterans Fear PTSD Stigmas."

116 Provider Information Management System, "Veterans Fear PTSD Stigmas."

the civilian world has been diagnosed with PTSD,[117] and as holistic therapies improve, the ability to control and resolve PTSD is improving. The stigma persists, though, and it hurts good people.

We need a better understanding of the military and veteran communities when considering opportunities for job placement. Without that understanding, veterans will lack employment and the ability to develop a career in the civilian world. Unemployment, financial ruin, self-medication to cope, depression, even suicide or run-ins with the law can follow if a future is not guaranteed. We need the civilian world to understand that a moment of compassion and support at work can alter that trajectory.

The stigma isn't just external; it's internal too. Military culture prizes strength and self-reliance. Many veterans fear admitting they need help or accommodations, lest they be seen as weak or (that dreaded word) "broken." Our Guardians often would rather tough it out alone than be labeled disabled or needy. While humility is admirable, it can be harmful when it stops someone from accessing resources or communicating their needs to an employer. So, we have a vicious cycle: Employers hesitate to ask or accommodate, and Guardians hesitate to tell or ask, and both sides remain silent.

That silence is dangerous.

The Impact of Untreated TBI

The cumulative effect of untreated TBI on employment is significant. This condition is often seen as a veteran-specific disorder, but each year, over two million people who visit the ER are diagnosed with TBI and face comorbidities such as substance abuse, depression, and even

117 U.S. Department of Veterans Affairs, "How Common Is PTSD in Adults?," last modified March 26, 2025, https://www.ptsd.va.gov/understand/common/common_adults.asp.

suicidal thoughts. The Americans with Disabilities Act (ADA) mandates workplace accommodations for these injuries, which can be as simple as adjusting lighting and noise levels.

Any person with an unaddressed brain injury is at significantly higher risk of self-medicating with drugs or alcohol, which, of course, can derail employment. But here's the hopeful flip side. If you have a clear path and you have an employment opportunity and you're getting treated for your TBI, you don't get on that substance. Work itself can be therapeutic, providing purpose, if coupled with proper treatment and understanding.

The key is identifying the TBI and accommodating it. In years past, many Guardians I saw were mislabeled as malingerers or written off because their injury was invisible. Thankfully, we have made progress in acknowledging TBI in the medical field since those early years of the war. But in the workplace, awareness is still lacking.

I often tell employers that accommodating a brain-injured veteran doesn't require heroics or huge expense. Sometimes, it's as simple as adjusting the environment. Minor adjustments, such as providing a quieter workspace, flexible breaks, and written checklists to aid memory, can make all the difference for a veteran with TBI.

By employing veterans with such injuries and listening to their needs, you prevent that person from spiraling downward to the point of being unemployable, homeless, and a staggering statistic of death by suicide. It's truly preventative maintenance for a human being. The return on investment for such understanding is immense.

You keep a valuable employee, and you quite possibly save a life or a family from tragedy. As our Guardians are strengthened, so are our companies, communities, and nation. Not enough employers know this. A veteran with cognitive issues might simply be labeled slow or not a good fit and quietly terminated elsewhere.

Untreated or unaccommodated TBI thus acts like a hidden anchor weighing veterans down in their job hunt and job performance. It is intimately tied to the stigma issue as well. A veteran may hide their TBI-related struggles out of fear, leading colleagues to misinterpret mistakes or mood swings. Conversely, an employer might notice something "off" and jump to conclusions without realizing it's a medical issue that can be managed.

This is why education is so crucial. If an employer understands that TBI might manifest as, say, slower processing of complex instructions, they can adjust training methods rather than assume the veteran is incapable. That patience and flexibility, often second nature in the military where you never leave a comrade behind, can be rare in the fast-paced civilian work culture. But it's exactly what's needed.

Toward an Inclusive Future

The current employment landscape for veterans is a mix of progress and problems. We've made headway in reducing joblessness and acknowledging invisible wounds, but veterans still face too many barriers. They exit service to a civilian world that often greets them with confusion, cliché, or cold bureaucracy instead of open arms.

Misperceptions label them as either heroes to be honored symbolically or as damaged goods to be avoided, when in truth they are highly skilled, adaptable people eager to contribute if given the chance. A lack of support in translating their hard-earned skills leaves many veterans frustrated in low-paying jobs that don't utilize their talents. Meanwhile, fear and stigma around brain health and TBI lurk in the shadows of interviews and onboarding, complicating what should be a straightforward match of talent to opportunity.

Yet, I remain optimistic. I've seen what happens when the narrative changes, when employers and communities step up. When a business truly employs and not just hires a veteran, it's transformative. As we'll explore in the next chapter, there are shining examples of this being done right.

The challenges outlined in this chapter—cultural misunderstandings, skill translation issues, stigma, and unaddressed injuries—are very real. But they are also addressable. As a nation, we can no longer simply thank veterans for their service; we must also support their future.

That means educating ourselves about what it really means to go from combat to cubicle, tearing down the stigmas that keep myths alive, and building policy bridges, training bridges, and human bridges to usher these men and women into roles where they can thrive. The mission is clear: Just as we once trained them to be soldiers, we must now train our systems to welcome veterans as valuable civilians. Anything less is a failure to complete the promise we made to them when they put on that uniform. We are on a mission, and that mission is to grant each veteran a future worthy of their past.

CHAPTER 11

FROM HIRING TO EMPLOYING

In the previous chapter, I described how many companies boast about hiring veterans but fail to truly integrate and retain them. This phenomenon boils down to a critical insight: Hiring a veteran is not the same as employing one. The distinction may sound semantic, but it's profound.

Hiring is about filling a quota or a short-term slot, whereas employing is about investing in a person's long-term growth and success within your organization. Too often, companies have chased the optics of veteran hiring without putting in the work to support those veterans post-hire. On Capitol Hill and in press releases, we hear numbers of vets hired, but we rarely hear how many are still there a year later or thriving in their roles.

Thankfully, some leaders do understand this difference deeply, and they are changing the game. In this chapter, I highlight successful employment models and give voice to the people creating them—the employers and advocates who are showing what works and why. At the forefront is my friend Bruce Daniels.

If you had told me years ago that one of the most innovative veteran employment programs I'd encounter would be at a car dealership, I might have been skeptical. Yet Bruce Daniels, who runs several Honda dealerships in the Columbus, Ohio area, has built what I consider the gold standard of employing veterans and others in need.

I first met Daniels decades ago when I was the medical director of Honda of America, and he was the go-to guy for anything automotive in the community. Over time, I learned he was more than a savvy businessman. He was a patriot with a heart for service. Daniels saw the struggles local veterans were having finding decent jobs and decided to do something radical and create a Technician Development Program that trains and employs veterans, as well as young people, and even those recovering from addiction, in automotive careers from the ground up.

This program, informally called the Future School of Drive, flips the script on traditional hiring. Instead of demanding experience or letting veterans fend for themselves in training, Bruce's team provides the education. They bring in candidates with little or no automotive background and pay them for their training, provide a starter tool kit, on-the-job experience, and a guaranteed job at a good wage.

Daniels proudly shared the details with me. After about sixty days of classroom and hands-on training, graduates start as entry-level technicians (M-techs), earning around $40,000 a year. From there, they can move up the ranks to C-tech, B-tech, and A-tech and potentially reach earnings of $100,000+ within five years as master technicians. That is a true career path. Importantly, the program doesn't require any state funding or gimmicky incentives.

What's remarkable is not just the training, but the philosophy behind it. Daniels and his colleagues approached this as more than a pipeline for workers and saw it as an opportunity to shape people.

"The goal of the program is to develop good people in a world that desperately needs good people," Daniels shared. Think about that. They sell and service cars, yes, but that's not who they are. Who they are is a company that develops good people. Profit is necessary, and employing good people is a way of guaranteeing profit.

The training classes at Daniels's Performance Honda include a mix of participants. Some fresh out of high school, some veterans, some folks overcoming personal challenges. Suppose ten students start a class. Maybe seven will quickly grasp the material, and three will struggle. In a typical corporate training scenario, those three might be deemed not a good fit and shown the door.

However, Daniels's program consciously fosters the sense of camaraderie and mission that veterans crave. The veterans quickly find friends and mentors who say, "Hey, we've got your back. You belong here."

The results speak volumes. Performance Honda's tech training program has dozens of graduates in good jobs, some within the company and some placed at other businesses.

Guardians Helping Guardians

One of these graduates is Dave Hartman, whom I introduced in the last chapter. Transitioning from his time in the Navy back to civilian life, Hartman began in a tire shop and steadily built a career in the automotive industry, working with major brands such as Honda, Mercedes, and Lexus before moving into management.

That path eventually led him to the Performance Automotive Network, where his life intersected with Daniels. Under Daniels's leadership, Hartman was given the opportunity to help design and now lead Honda Marysville's training department. Together, they share a vision of not just hiring workers but developing people—particularly young students and veterans—by equipping them with technical skills, mentoring, and a sense of purpose.

Today, Hartman continues his service by building futures. Hartman shared that even if they train one hundred people and only two end up working for their dealerships, "We change the lives of ninety-eight for the better elsewhere." That generosity of spirit is rare in business, and I truly believe their model is a template for others. It proves that if you give our Guardians real opportunities and support, they will excel. It also proves that doing so can be profitable in the long run.

Hartman's journey from tank crewman to service technician to manager and now head of training is inspiring on its own. But what strikes me most is how grounded and mission-focused he is in helping other veterans succeed. Initially a self-described punk kid who only thrived in the structured military environment, Hartman found purpose through learning a trade and being part of a civilian team. Now, he actively reaches out to young Guardians and even high schoolers to guide them.

In our conversations, Hartman emphasized that not every veteran will become a mechanic or work at a dealership, and that's OK. "The beauty of it is, yes, that's what we want. But we want to train them, we want to place them, we want to give them a path," he explained. I love that mentality: Even if we can't hire them, we will set them on the right path somewhere else. That is the voice of an advocate.

People like Hartman illustrate the difference between a company that merely hires veterans and one that truly embraces them. He told me about the camaraderie in the trades and how it can fulfill the longing veterans have for that "unit" feeling. So, in his recruiting pitches at job fairs or schools, he doesn't just talk about salary; he talks about finding brotherhood in the civilian world.

Many veterans leave service feeling that nothing will ever match the closeness or sense of purpose they had in uniform. Hartman shows them that a workshop or a work crew can offer a version of that: a team, a mission, and an end-of-day feeling of accomplishment at the end of every job.

In fact, every successful model I've seen includes some element of peer mentorship or support network. Whether it's formal, such as a veteran employee resource group at a big corporation, or informal, such as pairing new veteran hires with a buddy who's been in the company for a while, this support dramatically improves outcomes. Guardians trust other Guardians. They're more likely to open up about struggles to someone who "speaks the language."

Daniels's organization is teeming with veterans at all levels, so a new hire immediately has a tribe. That's something any company, even those without a big veteran program, can emulate. If you have even two or three veterans on staff, encourage them to form a support system for incoming vets. It could be as simple as a lunch meetup or a Slack channel, but it matters.

In 2012, Mike Musto, CEO of U.S. Pavement Services and a true patriot, began a campaign to buy only American products and services. "I felt this was the right thing to do to support our country,"[118] says Musto. After sharing the news about the new "Buy American" campaign with employees, everybody thought it was a great idea. There was a concern that it would be difficult to do. That wasn't the case.

By the end of that year, U.S. Pavement Services succeeded in its goal and began using "Buy American" in its marketing. Musto then invited numerous other pavement companies throughout the country to join in. It was a highlight at the National Pavement Expo that year.

Next, with the GWOT being waged for over a decade, Musto began a program of employing veterans, including those who had sustained significant injuries. Although Musto is not a veteran, he has always been a strong supporter in the true sense of the word. "I am so grateful to veterans for everything that they sacrificed and selflessly serving our

118 Mike Musto, interview by Chrisanne Gordon, May 29, 2025.

nation all over the world to make this country free. We need to pay them back", says Musto. U.S. Pavement Services began a campaign to employ our Guardians. He challenged other pavement companies throughout the country to employ at least one veteran in 2015. Mike accommodated and placed his trust in Steve Bohn of the 101st Airborne Division of the Army. Steve was seriously wounded in Afghanistan by a suicide bomber, and many of his colleagues didn't survive. Not only did Musto employ Steve, but he also incorporated Steve's suggestions to set the tone for the entire veterans' employment program.

"Good employees bring good karma,"[119] and U.S. Pavement Services grew because of this initiative. The campaigns were great for our Guardians and for the businesses. Musto states, "It's a no-brainer. You do the right thing in supporting our veterans and our country, and you get more business because of it." Musto then organized a yearly Boston Red Sox game, hosting three hundred veterans and their families. The joy that it brought to veterans and the fans was truly amazing.

Besides giving back by supporting veterans, Musto states that there are many reasons why companies should employ veterans. They are dependable, dedicated, disciplined, and technically advanced. Veterans have strong leadership skills that have been battle-tested, and they are true team players who have been well-trained. Veterans should be considered by every company.

U.S. Pavement Services continues to employ and support veterans, even after Musto's retirement. His values and support for our veterans and our country continue throughout the pavement industry. Steve Bohn has come a long way since sustaining severe wounds in Afghanistan and recovering from many years of surgery. He is now a veterans support officer for seven towns in Massachusetts, continuing to assist others who served our nation.

---

119 Musto, interview.

"Working with and supporting veterans has been one of the most satisfying and rewarding experiences in my life." —**Mike Musto**

What Works

Based on my conversation with leaders such as Bruce Daniels and Mike Musto, let's distill what makes it work and highlight a few other shining examples.

MISSION AND PURPOSE OVER PROFIT

Successful models give Guardians a mission. In Daniels's program, the mission might be "become the best technician you can be" or simply the daily mission of fixing cars as part of a team. They tap into that intrinsic motivation veterans have. Other companies do this by aligning veterans with roles that have a clear sense of purpose.

Profit is not the sole driver. It's a byproduct. Ironically, by not focusing solely on profit, these models often end up being more profitable because of higher productivity and lower turnover.

TRAINING AND EDUCATION

Virtually every success story I've seen involves some form of training or education pathway. It can be on-the-job training, such as at the dealership, or formal programs like Hiring Our Heroes corporate fellowships. The key is acknowledging that veterans may need to learn industry-specific skills and that investing in that learning upfront pays off.

Many companies partner with community colleges or vocational schools to create veteran cohorts in trades like plumbing, HVAC, or cybersecurity. These programs work because they bridge the gap, translating military skills into civilian credentials in a supportive environment, often with other vets.

MENTORSHIP AND PEER SUPPORT

In any effective model, there are people ensuring the veteran doesn't feel alone. Sometimes, it's a formal mentor and buddy system. Sometimes, it's a veteran affinity group inside a company.

I know of a manufacturing firm that pairs each new veteran hire with an older veteran in the company for their first year. Or tech companies where veteran employees have a private messaging channel to share advice. These connections provide moral support and practical tips. They also create a mini community that can advocate internally if a veteran employee hits a snag. The importance of community cannot be overstated. It is what turns a job into a supportive environment.

FLEXIBILITY AND UNDERSTANDING

Employers succeeding with Guardians show flexibility in policies and understanding in management. Daniels's willingness not to fire the PTSD-affected employee and instead to support him is a perfect example. Another would be companies that offer flexible schedules for veterans going to VA appointments or therapy sessions. Some progressive employers even offer additional leave for guard/reserve duties beyond the legal minimum, understanding that serving part-time is part of who that military member is.

In training, as Hartman said, it means not giving up on someone who learns differently. In day-to-day work, it might mean recognizing that a veteran's direct communication style isn't rudeness and coaching the team around that difference. I recall Daniels mentioning that one challenge they sift through is finding those who are truly serious about a long-term career.

He's flexible on background, but he expects commitment. Flexibility is not the same as coddling; it's about meeting someone halfway.

The best programs hold Guardians to high standards but also give them the tools and grace to meet those standards.

HOLISTIC SUPPORT

Some models extend beyond the job itself. Daniels pointed out that one benefit of employing a veteran in a good job is that they'll have health insurance and fewer hoops to jump through for care. A veteran working for a stable company might be able to get, say, mental health counseling through an employer benefits plan right away rather than sitting on a VA waitlist.

In essence, a solid job can bring a veteran into a supportive ecosystem. A few large companies have recognized this and partner with veteran service organizations to provide wraparound support, including financial literacy classes, family support, or counseling. At a policy level, some advocate that companies hiring vets should coordinate with the VA or local nonprofits to ensure the vet's whole well-being is addressed. Truly employing a veteran often means recognizing they might need more than a paycheck and require mentorship, health support, or simply patience to adjust to the civilian workforce.

LEADERSHIP BUY-IN AND CULTURE

Lastly, none of this works without genuine buy-in from the top and a culture that values service. Bruce Daniels exemplifies top-down commitment. He set the tone that "helping veterans is who we are." However, I've also seen bottom-up influence, where a few passionate employees can start a movement within a company.

For instance, a group of veteran employees can propose a hiring initiative to HR, or a local manager can decide to actively recruit vets to their team and demonstrate success, which then influences higher-ups. However, leadership eventually has to endorse it for it to truly flourish company-wide.

More than a Job

What these insights boil down to is that truly employing a veteran means seeing them as a whole person with a future, not just a past. I've been in rooms in Washington, DC, where advocates share stories. A veteran who was aimless and suicidal until a manager took him under his wing in an apprenticeship. A female veteran who struggled to reconnect until she got a job at a veteran-founded company where she finally felt understood. Companies that experimented with reverse mentorship to break down culture gaps.

The common thread is human connection and high expectations. Treat a veteran as a valued team member from day one, and they will usually exceed your expectations. Veterans can actually raise the performance bar for everyone else, given the right environment. I've seen factories and offices where, once a critical mass of veterans was hired, overall punctuality and teamwork improved—not through coercion, but by example.

As Daniels noted, it's not just about helping veterans, it's about finding the right veterans who are ready to succeed and putting them in the right seats. He observed that one challenge is sifting out who is truly serious about the opportunity. Some people, whether high schoolers or vets, might not yet be in the mindset to commit to a career path.

Similarly, not every veteran will thrive in every industry. A key to successful employment is aligning a vet's interests and passions with the job. That implies matching Guardians to roles that fit them. In our context, that often means figuring out what the veteran wants to do, not just plugging them into a generic "veteran job." One size does not fit all. The company should be interested in what veterans themselves are interested in doing. That is vital.

When you give a Guardian a purpose, a plan, and a partner, you unleash their potential. Bruce Daniels gave them a purpose (service through work), a plan (training and career path), and partners (mentors like Hartman). It's a formula that others can replicate. Indeed, I hope reading about this inspires more employers to say, "We can do something like that." It doesn't have to be on the same scale.

Not every business can start a full training academy, but perhaps they can start a veteran internship program or commit to hiring a certain number of veterans and supporting them with mentors. It is doable, and it's worth it.

CHAPTER 12

FROM PROMISES TO ACTION

As we've explored, Guardians navigating the civilian employment world face systemic obstacles but also have incredible potential to enrich our workforce. We've heard the personal stories, seen models of success, and identified where things often go wrong. Now, it's time to talk solutions. What needs to change to transform veteran employment from a patchwork of good intentions into a reliable, supportive system that yields meaningful careers?

In this final chapter, I want to offer some clear, actionable recommendations drawn from the voices and experiences we've discussed, and my own perspective after years of advocacy. These recommendations span policy changes, employer practices, and cultural shifts, because it truly is a shared mission. Each has a role to play in building a future where every veteran has the opportunity to thrive in the workplace.

A recurring theme has been transition—that fragile period when a service member becomes a civilian. We've seen that this handoff is where many problems originate. When the DOW begins collaborating for a more successful handoff to the civilian world, the futures of our former military members will be guaranteed. This includes accepting the wounds of war; documenting them in a medical record given at military discharge, along with a plan for healthcare, education, and employment. We must change the system immediately to ensure that our military members, when discharged, no longer spend years having to prove they have an injury or illness related to service. With accurate documentation of injuries and illnesses and with coordination of post-military care, we can improve the futures of our Guardians beginning immediately.

That must change at the policy level. Equally, companies need to change how they recruit, hire, and retain veterans, moving from superficial "Thank you for your service, here's a job" approaches to substantive career development and support. And socially, we need to eradicate stigma and update perceptions of veterans. Moreover, we should foster a culture that values military skills as assets and encourages veterans to be proud of their background, as 97 percent of veterans believe they should be.[120]

Policy Recommendations

In the spirit of being data-informed and mission-driven, I'll outline specific changes under three areas—policy, employers, and community—followed by concrete steps to implement them. These recommendations are not pie-in-the-sky ideas. They come from what we've learned through hard experience and from the successful blueprints described in chapter 11.

They are, as Bruce Daniels would say, mostly common sense, and many are little things that can add up to a big impact. It's time to move from admitting the problem to actually fixing it. We owe our Guardians no less than a concerted effort to grant them the future they deserve, and in doing so, we will strengthen our economy and our national character.

120 Provider Information Management System, "Veterans Fear PTSD Stigmas."

Overhaul the Military-to-Civilian Transition Program

The current TAP, while useful, is not sufficient. We need a more comprehensive handoff from the DOW to civilian life. One option is to implement a transitional bridging program in which service members spend at least four to eight weeks before discharge in an internship or training program with potential civilian employers or in an on-base skill course.

Congress and the DOW should mandate and fund this as part of out-processing. For example, units at major bases could partner with companies to set up on-site career training academies. A Guardian might spend their last month in uniform learning A+, Network+ certifications for IT, or welding skills, or even doing a trial apprenticeship.

During this time, their full pay and benefits would continue uninterrupted, and they would transition gradually, building civilian skills and networking before they need a job. This approach would address both skill translation and anxiety about the unknown. It's essentially an expanded TAP with teeth. Not just resume-writing classes, but actual skill and job placement opportunities.

Hold the DOW Accountable for Transition Outcomes

It's time to end the DOW's "scot-free" pass and handoff to the VA regarding what happens to troops after service. One action is to institute a system in which each branch of the military is required to track and report on the one-year outcomes of its separating service members and tie a portion of command evaluations or funding to successful transitions.

This could mean, for example, the Army must report that some percentage of Guardians who left in 2025 are employed or in school by 2026. If a branch consistently underperforms, budget for transition programs is increased, or leadership is pressed to improve the TAP. Essentially, we should make transition assistance a core mission of the DOW, not just the VA. Additionally, service medical records and rehab information for injuries (especially TBI and PTSD) should seamlessly be transferred to the VA and accessible to the veteran and any future employer programs with consent.

Incentivize Employment Outcomes, Not Just Hiring

Federal and state governments should revise their incentive structures for companies. Currently, companies can receive tax credits, such as the Work Opportunity Tax Credit, for hiring veterans. However, this does not guarantee long-term success. One action step is to create or reform incentives so that tax credits or public recognition rewards are tied to retention and career progression. It is not enough to hire; the goal is to employ.

For example, consider offering a larger tax credit to veteran employees who stay twelve months or more and receive a promotion or raise rather than providing the same credit on the day of hire. Another approach is that public veteran-friendly employer ratings could incorporate retention rates.

We could ask companies to report how many vets they hired and how many remain after a year. Only those above a certain retention threshold earn top rankings or government contracts preference. Essentially, shift the conversation from “thank you for hiring vets” to “thank you for investing in our Guardians’ future.” This also discourages the churn-and-burn model we decried.

Expand Education and Training Benefits for New Careers

The GI Bill already provides educational funding, but not all veterans want a four-year degree. Many need faster, targeted training for trades or certifications. One option is to enhance and promote programs such as the Veteran Rapid Retraining Assistance Program or create new ones that fund short-term vocational training in high-demand fields, including tech, healthcare, and skilled trades.

Additionally, as noted, consider models from allies. Australia's Gold Card concept gives vets free access to healthcare and education for a period. We might not replicate it exactly, but we could ensure every honorably discharged veteran gets, for example, up to two years of free community college or technical school on top of the GI Bill, which could then be saved for later use or higher degrees.

This would facilitate re-skilling for those whose military job doesn't have a direct civilian equivalent. It also eases the transition by giving veterans structured environments to adapt to civilian student life, which parallels the transition to civilian work life. Congress can fund this by expanding GI Bill eligibility or creating state-level veteran scholarships. The payoff is a more skilled veteran workforce ready to enter new industries.

Healthcare and Mental Health as Part of Employment Strategy

Policy should recognize that untreated health issues (especially TBI/PTSD) hinder employment. This could be done through integrating VA healthcare with employment initiatives. For example, develop a Veteran Work Ready health assessment that, with the veteran's consent, evaluates any functional impairments and suggests workplace accommodations or treatments before they start a new job. The ADA would cover these accommodations as necessary for every workplace.

This could be offered in the final months of service or immediately post-discharge. Also, fund grants for companies to implement brain health support programs for veteran employees, perhaps via the Department of Labor. If an employer hires a veteran with TBI/PTSD, make it easy for them to get free advice from VA counselors on how to adjust to the workplace.

Another policy idea is to require that any large employer receiving federal contracts have a basic veteran support plan in place. This leverages procurement policy to spread best practices. Ultimately, by treating health and employment as linked, we cut down on the costly cycle of unemployment, worsening health, and higher VA costs.

Employer Actions

When it comes to employing Guardians, the conversation must move beyond symbolic gestures and one-off hiring pushes. Too many employers treat veteran hiring as a box to check rather than as a sustained, strategic investment. Veterans bring discipline, leadership, and adaptability that can transform a workforce, but unlocking that value requires more than just recruitment. It means building dedicated pipelines, shaping veteran-friendly workplace cultures, adopting flexible policies, leveraging their unique strengths, and tracking progress with intention.

The following sections outline practical ways companies, whether large corporations or small businesses, can move from occasional hires to a holistic approach that cultivates veteran talent, supports their transition, and ultimately strengthens the organization as a whole.

Develop Veteran Talent Pipelines

Employers should shift from sporadic veteran hiring efforts to building continuous pipelines. This means companies, large or small, can partner with military bases, local National Guard units, or veteran organizations to identify candidates early. For instance, create internships or SkillBridge programs to bring transitioning service members in-house before they leave service.

Many companies have had success here, and it's time to expand it. Manufacturing companies could start an apprenticeship specifically for vets. IT companies can host a coding bootcamp for veterans and hire those who complete it. The idea is to stop thinking of veteran hiring as plugging a hole and start thinking of it as cultivating high-potential talent.

Others can emulate this by creating their own version of a training academy or by supporting nonprofits that do training. Remember that over 60 percent of vets are underemployed, partly because of a lack of industry-specific credentials,[121] so employers can fill that gap by providing the training and certification pathways. Not only does this create skilled employees, but it also engenders loyalty.

Foster a Veteran-Friendly Workplace Culture

It's not enough to hire Guardians. The workplace must make them feel included and valued. Employers should implement veteran affinity groups or mentorship programs. As discussed, pairing new veteran hires with a mentor, preferably another veteran or a supportive senior employee, for the first year can drastically improve adjustment and retention.

121 Due, "America Solved Veterans' Unemployment Within a Decade."

Provide cultural competency training for nonveteran managers. Essentially, educate your staff on military culture basics and the value veterans bring. Something as simple as a lunch-and-learn session, in which veterans share their experiences, can help break down stereotypes. Companies such as Starbucks and JPMorganChase have veteran networks that organize such events and even assist in recruiting.[122]

Adopt Flexible HR Policies for Guardians' Needs

Some veterans may need minor accommodations or schedule flexibility, especially in the early transition period. Employers should review their HR policies to ensure they accommodate military-related needs. This includes time off for VA appointments or counseling without stigma; minor accommodations for lighting, noise, and training; or even bringing counseling and rehab in-house to be delivered during work hours.

You could also implement a confidential way for a veteran hire to disclose a TBI or PTSD if they choose to do so and request accommodations. Then, be ready to provide for them, whether it's noise-cancelling headphones, a slightly modified schedule, or allowing a service dog at work. These are generally low-cost adjustments. Managers should be trained that if a veteran is struggling, the first question is "How can we help?" rather than "What's wrong with them?"

Recognize and Leverage Guardians' Strengths

Employers should consciously leverage the qualities that make our Guardians unique to the work environment, for they have already proved their commitment to service. They should put Guardians in

122 Due, "America Solved Veterans' Unemployment Within a Decade."

roles where their leadership, teamwork, and mission focus shine. If you have a floundering project, consider a veteran to organize it. They've led teams in chaos before.

If you need reliability in shift work, a veteran will likely be punctual and accountable. Veterans sometimes feel out of place in a lax culture, so instead of the veteran having to lower their standards, encourage others to rise to theirs. Consider starting meetings on time and acknowledging the influence of your veteran team members. Create pathways for promotion for veterans. Many have leadership experience by their mid-twenties, leading dozens of people or managing millions in equipment.

Don't pigeonhole them in low roles because they lack civilian seniority. Fast-track them when appropriate, as they did at Honda Marysville, where vets can progress from entry M-tech to A-tech in five years based on skill, not just tenure. Listen to their suggestions, as did Mike Musto at U.S. Pavement Services. Some companies have new veteran hires undergo brief training alongside other employees to cross-pollinate skills. The veteran learns corporate skills, while the others focus on military teamwork. This leverages strengths both ways.

MEASURE SUCCESS AND ADJUST

Finally, employers should treat their veteran employment initiative as a strategic imperative that is measured and refined. Track metrics such as veteran retention rate, performance, promotion rate, and satisfaction via surveys. If something's not working, dive in to find out why.

It might be that mentorship needs strengthening, or the role wasn't a fit. Solicit feedback from your veteran employees and make them stakeholders in improving the program. Many companies that succeed have a dedicated program manager for veteran initiatives or, at the very least, a task force that meets regularly.

If you lead a smaller business, you, as the owner or manager, might take this on personally. A great approach is simply to sit down with each of your veteran employees periodically and ask how it's going and what could be better. By measuring outcomes, you avoid assumptions.

Perhaps you thought your onboarding was solid, but vets still felt lost. Their feedback will guide you to add, for example, a two-week buddy shadowing. In essence, apply the same continuous improvement mindset you would to any other business function.

Community and Social Change

Veteran employment is not just a workforce issue but a cultural and societal challenge that requires a broad mindset shift. While many employers and communities have taken steps to support Guardians, the focus often remains fragmented or rooted in outdated perceptions. What's needed now is a holistic approach that elevates veterans as vital contributors to our economy and society.

This means tackling stereotypes head-on, creating support networks, reframing employment as a value exchange rather than charity, empowering veterans to seek help and aim high, and fostering collaboration across public and private sectors. The following recommendations outline how each of these pillars can help build a more sustainable and impactful path forward for veterans transitioning into civilian life.

PUBLIC AWARENESS AND EDUCATION CAMPAIGNS

As a society, we need to dismantle outdated stereotypes and highlight the successes of veterans. This might include launching campaigns to showcase modern veterans' stories. Normalize the idea that veterans are diverse, skilled, and adaptable. Just as Vietnam vets battled the "damaged goods" stigma, post-9/11 vets battle the TBI/invisible wound stereotype.

We must continue to publicize facts such as "over 80 percent of veterans do not have PTSD."[123] We must also remember that brain health issues are prevalent in military and nonmilitary prospective employees, and every company should have policies to assist accommodation and recovery.

Encourage news outlets, social media, and Hollywood to portray veterans in nuanced ways—not just as the troubled vet or the hero vet, but as everyday citizens who bring unique experiences. On a local level, communities can hold veteran job fairs that double as education events for employers. The more employers hear success stories and understand the reward-benefit ratio is amazing for the investment, the more they will proactively seek veteran talent.

GUARDIANS NETWORKING AND SUPPORT GROUPS

Guardians themselves can take action by leaning on each other and guiding those who come after them. Encourage the formation of local veteran mentorship networks where employed veterans help recently separated folks navigate the job market. Many cities have "Veterans in Business" or veteran professional meetups. Those are great and can be expanded. Also, online platforms have veteran mentor programs, and we should promote these to all separating service members. A peer saying "Try this career" or "I know someone at *X* company" can open doors that formal programs might miss.

Social support is crucial, too. Family readiness groups on bases should extend to post-separation, connecting spouses and vets in new communities so they don't feel isolated. Community colleges with high

123 Provider Information Management System, "Veterans Fear PTSD Stigmas."

veteran attendance can host support circles for student veterans and link them with local employers. Essentially, create a fabric of community that catches veterans as they transition, so if one approach isn't working out, they have somewhere to turn besides despair.

EMPHASIZE VALUE, NOT CHARITY

Both messaging and practice must treat veteran employment as a mutually beneficial proposition, not a favor to the veteran.

Employing a veteran isn't just helping them; it's strengthening America. So, challenge communities to think of veteran underemployment as wasted talent that hurts us all. For example, if 60 percent of vets are underemployed,[124] that's a brain drain and leadership void in our economy. Publicize that. Also, highlight the companies doing it right and call out those just paying lip service.

The public can influence this by choosing to patronize businesses known to treat veterans well. Community leaders can create Veteran-Friendly Employer of the Year awards to encourage competition in doing right by vets. Social pressure and recognition can push companies to step up their game from just hiring to genuinely employing veterans.

ENCOURAGE GUARDIANS TO SEEK HELP AND AIM HIGH

On the veterans' side, a cultural change is needed to reduce the stigma of asking for assistance and to encourage ambition in the civilian sector. Many veterans initially feel they don't deserve special help, or they undersell themselves in jobs far below their capabilities.

Veteran service organizations and counselors often reinforce that using benefits isn't a handout; it's earned. We should tell veterans that it's not a weakness to seek guidance on their resume or go to therapy

124 Due, "America Solved Veterans' Unemployment Within a Decade."

for their combat stress. It is a sign of strength to prepare yourself fully for the next mission.

In practical terms, community programs might include career coaching workshops specifically for veterans where they practice translating their experiences into civilian language. Also, encourage vets to be bold. If they led troops, they shouldn't hesitate to apply for a manager role. If they handled complex machinery, consider advanced manufacturing jobs.

Essentially, instill confidence that they can compete at any level. As one survey indicated, 92 percent of veterans believe their military experience makes them better employees.[125] That confidence needs to be shown outwardly, not hidden. Society can help by affirming those aspirations. Mentorship programs that pair vets with executives to learn corporate ropes, and entrepreneurship training for vets with business ideas. These show that we expect great things from veterans, not just to get by but to lead in civilian life as they did in service.

PUBLIC–PRIVATE COLLABORATION AND SUSTAINED MISSION FOCUS

Finally, a broad societal recommendation: Treat veteran employment as a national mission requiring the unified effort we give to other major initiatives. We saw after 2011 that a combination of companies, government, and nonprofits can move the needle, when they rallied to reduce unemployment.[126]

We need to rekindle that coalition, this time targeting quality of employment and underemployment. One way to do this is to establish a National Veterans Employment Coalition that includes Fortune 500 CEOs, small business owners, veterans' organizations, educational

125 Provider Information Management System, "Veterans Fear PTSD Stigmas."

126 Due, "America Solved Veterans' Unemployment Within a Decade."

institutions, and government agencies. They would meet, share data and best practices, and coordinate initiatives.

With a clear goal, each sector can align its efforts. The coalition can also push for needed legislative changes with one voice. Essentially, maintain momentum and accountability, and don't let veteran employment fall off the radar, especially when overall unemployment is low. Because, as a RAND study said, "it is too early to simply declare 'mission accomplished' on veteran employment."[127] We must evolve the mission.

Resurrect a Hero, Strengthen a Nation

Implementing these changes will take commitment, resources, and a shift in mindset, but none are beyond our reach. In fact, many are extensions of what we're already learning from successful pockets of excellence. It's a matter of scaling up those successes and not tolerating mediocrity or failure in how we support our Guardians.

The cost of inaction is measured in more than dollars. It's broken families, wasted human capital, and a moral failing toward those who served. Conversely, the benefits of getting this right are immense: Not only do our Guardians thrive, but employers gain outstanding talent, and communities benefit from leaders and role models.

Our Guardians are, as I often say, the 1 percent who did what 99 percent did not. They volunteered to serve, to give their lives, if necessary, to protect our freedoms. And they deserve the full measure of opportunities those freedoms encompass. Anyone who has sustained a TBI can attest that, in the recovery, you learn to adjust to a new brain, a new you. In essence, a new brain is resurrected from the old—hence our motto at the RLF is "Resurrect a Hero, Strengthen a Nation."

127 Due, "America Solved Veterans' Unemployment Within a Decade."

They've already proven their dedication, adaptability, and resilience. Now, it's on us to harness those qualities in their civilian lives. That starts by removing unnecessary roadblocks and putting in place supports that we know work. We also must honor their service in practical ways, not just with words.

I want to close with a vision of what success looks like. It's a vision where a young woman leaving the Army has multiple job offers in hand before she hangs up her uniform because companies scouted her leadership talent early. It's a vision where a Marine with a TBI doesn't hide it in shame at a new job but openly communicates with a trained supervisor who adjusts the role so that the Marine excels and everyone sees that, brain injury or not, they're a top performer. These measures will assist in brain recovery to the new normal of success in the civilian world.

It's seeing not just reduced veteran unemployment and underemployment rates, but also increased job satisfaction and fulfillment rates. It's hearing employers talk about veterans as a cornerstone of their talent strategy, not check-the-box outreach. It's veterans rising to top executive positions or running successful businesses and reaching back to pull the next ones up. It's also a future where the average American understands what veterans bring—service above self.

The mission to get there will require steady effort. But as I've learned in this journey, when you work toward brain injury recovery or veteran transition, it's best to journey with a friend and keep your spirit strong. We have millions of friends on this mission. Every veteran and every supporter is an ally in the cause.

And we have reason for a strong spirit. We know what works; we know the character of the men and women we're fighting for. They fought for us; now it's our turn. With grounded practical steps, data to guide us, and emotional resolve, we can ensure that every veteran finds not just a job, but a welcome home and a purpose in the civilian workforce. That is a future worth fighting for, and together, we will make it a reality.

Together, we can build the systems that grant our Guardians a future as bright and dignified as their service to us has been.

CONCLUSION

We stand at a crossroads. On one side is the status quo, with bureaucratic delays, fractured systems, and a culture that applauds service but too often abandons the servant. On the other side is a nation that refuses to let its Guardians walk alone. The stories and solutions you have read throughout these pages prove that change is not only possible but already happening in pockets across America. The question is whether we will scale it with urgency and resolve.

The call is not limited to policymakers or institutions. It belongs to *every* citizen. If you are an employer, open your doors and see veterans not as charity hires, but as leaders who will strengthen your workforce. If you are an educator, build bridges that translate battlefield skills into classroom success. If you are a neighbor, extend compassion and connection that make reintegration possible. And if you are a veteran yourself, know that your voice and your story are powerful tools to reshape the system for those who follow.

Circling back to Margaret Mead's famous statement that I quoted in the introduction:

> Never doubt that a small group of thoughtful, committed citizens can change the world. Indeed, it is the only thing that ever has.[128]

---

128 Mead, "Never doubt that a small group of thoughtful, committed citizens can change the world."

Imagine what will be gained when these individual acts combine into a movement. A veteran no longer waits months for care but receives it immediately. A student veteran no longer feels like an outsider but becomes the leader of her class. A father returning from war is not broken by isolation but restored by community. This vision is within reach, but it requires us to choose action over apathy, investment over indifference.

The mission is clear. The time is now. And the responsibility belongs to us all.

EPILOGUE

G*uarding Our Guardians* is a remarkable and touching way to look and learn about the changes and needs of the men and women who have served and continue to serve our country—especially those living with unrecognized PTSD and traumatic brain injuries that too often lead to homelessness, unemployment, and suicide.

Too many of our Guardians are struggling in silence, their injuries invisible to those around them. Some have found themselves entangled in the criminal justice system, while others battle addiction or face barriers to employment and education—all because the care for PTSD and traumatic brain injuries was not taken seriously enough, soon enough. These veterans should not be forgotten, regardless of where they find themselves today.

Let us remember that because someone may look healthy and appear to be functioning fine, that person may be suffering from wounds that cannot be seen.

Our service men and women need and deserve adequate time to navigate from military life to civilian life. I believe that far more support than what's provided in boot camp is needed to prepare them for this transition—particularly in healthcare, education, and employment.

I want to thank Dr. Chrisanne Gordon for her dedication to this vitally important work. Her loyalty and determination to continue bringing TBI and PTSD to the forefront are priceless.

-Sandy Vorhies

AMVETS National First Vice Commander

ACKNOWLEDGMENTS

I would like to acknowledge all the amazing people who worked diligently to launch our book and our movement, *Guarding Our Guardians: Guaranteeing America's Veterans a Future from Deployment to Employment*.

This includes my co-author, Ezra Byer; the amazing team at Forbes Books; all our incredible experts; and especially our courageous veterans who continue to enlighten us on the true meaning of sacrifice and honor. A special acknowledgment goes to the eighth and ninth secretaries of Veterans Affairs, former Secretary Robert "Bob" McDonald and former Secretary David Shulkin, MD, who tirelessly continue advocating for our Guardians' futures.

www.ingramcontent.com/pod-product-compliance
Lightning Source LLC
LaVergne TN
LVHW012329100826
845148LV00017B/541

* 9 7 9 8 8 9 1 8 8 0 1 3 9 *